Published in 2007 by Highdown,
an imprint of Raceform Ltd
Compton, Newbury, Berkshire, RG20 6NL

A catalogue record for this book is available from the British Library.

ISBN: 978-1-905156-42-9

Designed by Adrian Morrish

Printed in Great Britain by Butler and Tanner

WHERE ARE

THEY

MATT ALLEN

Rediscovering over 100 football stars from the 70s, 80s & early 90s

NOW!

INTRODUCTION

A playground. Somewhere in Bromley. The early 1980s.

"Arthur Albiston?"
"Got…"
"Jan Molby?"
"Got…"
"A curling team shot of Coventry City with the corners peeled?"
"Need! Need! Need to finish the page!"

I'd hear it at playtime, whenever it was snowing or hailing. Friends – flicking through tattered sticker books – desperately trying to fill the blank spaces with mug shots of Eric Gates, Bobby Barnes, Mel Sterland and Garth Crooks (yes, even Garth Crooks).

The weather meant we couldn't run through the playground with my tattered Minerva Supreme ball, scoring goals like Mark Falco. Instead we swapped stickers and read *Roy Of The Rovers* in the canteen. Later in class, I'd dream of playing in front of the big crowds, like the fictional Ronnie Blake in Brian Glanville's novel, *Goalkeepers Are Different* (even though he was a goalie and I always played in midfield).

But back in break time (when it was raining or snowing) it was an aggressive trading floor of comics and collectibles. Some cards were more revered than others – Ossie Ardiles and his strange moustache in 1986/1987 (for comedy value); the glittering World Cup trophy card of 1982 (a badge of honour) and any pictures of Brazilian chain smoker, Socrates (because he was so cool).

Others held a more mystical quality. In Tony Galvin's fact file it was widely reported that Spurs' industrious winger was a football anomaly: he held a BA (hons) in Russian. For most kids around the age of 10, it was as if Galvin had been schooled in Klingon.

But like Saint And Greavsie, Adidas Tangos and Patrick boots, the names, haircuts and unusual facial hair were synonymous with professional football's most romantic era. An era where players didn't drive Baby Bentleys or swagger from London nightclubs in fur coats (unless they were Justin Fashanu). An era without half-baked autobiographies, wedding exclusives in *OK! Magazine* and WAGs. An era without *'image rights'*.

In those days, players on the telly looked like the neighbourhood milkman, not a Hollywood prima donna. And they were heroes in their own way. They didn't play for £20,000 a week, they played for the team. For the terraces. For the ultimate dream … Wembley, First Division glory or international recognition.

Where Are They Now? tracks down those heroes. Players and familiar football faces from a pre-Premiership era (and one or two who strayed into the big bucks during the latter stages of their career) and recalls their football milestones. Players that now bask in their former glories while selling wine, farming pigs or inventing TV game shows for a living. The 'Got, got. Need! Need!' collectibles of the playground.

Zip up the snorkel parka, it's time to catch up with the heroes of a forgotten era.

"Mark Chamberlain?"
"Got."
"Imre Varadi?"
"Got…"

MATT ALLEN, BALHAM, 2007.

1 RICKY VILLA

Quilmes (Argentina), San Martin de Tucuman (Argentina), Atletico de Tucuman (Argentina), Racing Club (Argentina), Tottenham Hotspur, Miami Strikers (USA), Deportivo Cali (Colombia)
• 1971-1989

BORN 18 August 1952

POSITION Midfielder

HONOURS Tottenham Hotspur: FA Cup Winner 1981

THEN Tottenham's louche midfielder with the Serpico beard and Don Henley haircut, Ricky Villa defined the term 'Wondergoal' with a mazy dribble in the 1981 FA Cup Final replay against Manchester City. With the game poised at 2-2, the Argentinean – who joined Spurs along with Ossie Ardiles following their 1978 World Cup glory – teased three defenders like a matador before tucking the ball under goalkeeper Joe Corrigan. The Falklands War later curtailed his English adventure – to avoid controversy, Villa missed the 1982 FA Cup Final against QPR and later admitted to watching the telly tearfully as his name was sung at Wembley. Following one more season at White Hart Lane he left for America and Miami Strikers in 1983.

NOW Currently retired, he lives in Argentina with his wife and four children. Villa often returns to England and can sometimes be spotted on the after dinner circuit, where he'll be forever remembered for that flash of FA Cup brilliance. 'Whenever I go back to London, people always want to talk about that goal,' he says. 'Even Arsenal fans! I am glad that so many people remember me for it, and I'm proud to be a little part of Wembley's history.' Last seen at White Hart Lane this year on a spoofed Che Guevara t-shirt.

Ricky Villa
TOTTENHAM HOTSPUR

2 JOHN WARK

Ipswich Town, Liverpool, Ipswich Town, Middlesbrough, Ipswich Town • 1975-1997

BORN 4 August 1957

POSITION Midfielder/defender

HONOURS Ipswich: FA Cup Winner 1978; UEFA Cup Winner 1981; Division Two Champions 1992. Liverpool: Division One Champions 1984, 1986

THEN Recognisable for his fearsome 'pimp' moustache, John Wark was ostensibly a two club man, with a spell a Boro' in between. He represented Ipswich Town during three separate stints and scooped the First Division title with Liverpool in 1984 and 1986. Having emerged under manager Bobby Robson at Portman Road, Wark carved his reputation as a talented attacking midfielder when Ipswich won the UEFA Cup in 1981. He was later named the PFA Players' Player of the Year (1981). In 1984, he moved to Anfield, joining a team big on facial hair, though his cult status was already ensured with two goals in the 1982 World Cup for Scotland and an appearance in the legendary football movie *Escape to Victory*, (1981) as POW Arthur Hayes, starring alongside Michael Caine and Sly Stallone. Sadly, his Liverpool career was dogged by injury and he later hopped to Portman Road (1988-1990) then Boro' (1990) and back to Ipswich (1991) again before retiring in 1997.

NOW Currently working for Ipswich Town's corporate hospitality department. Despite hitting 50, Wark refuses to hang up his boots, joining the likes of Gary Gillespie in the Liverpool Masters side. 'I play for a works team on Sundays, too,' he says. 'People recognise me all the time, though they ask me more questions about *Escape to Victory* than anything else.' He's even kept his trademarked moustache, now affectionately referred to as 'a Wark'. 'My hair's going a bit, but I've still got the 'tache,' he says. 'Everyone had them back then. Souness had a good one. And Rivelino had a brilliant moustache with droopy side bits. I think Steven Gerrard could get away with 'a Wark' today. He's a midfield general and you need a moustache to be a midfield general.'

John Wark
LIVERPOOL

3 NORMAN WHITESIDE

Manchester United, Everton • 1982-1990

BORN 7 May 1965

POSITION Striker

HONOURS Manchester United: FA Cup Winner 1983, 1985

THEN When Norman Whiteside scored the winner for Manchester United against Everton in the 1985 FA Cup Final – a swerving shot that curled around 'keeper, Neville Southall – the world seemed poised at his feet. He had already gone one better than Pelé by becoming the youngest player to appear in the World Cup finals (he was 17 when he played in Spain 1982). He was the youngest player to represent United since Duncan Edwards. He was also the youngest player to score in an FA Cup Final (against Brighton in 1983). But by the age of 26, Whiteside's career was in tatters. He was hindered by injuries and was off to Everton in 1989. Knee trouble eventually finished his career. 'It was a bad day giving up football,' he says. 'You mope around for a couple of weeks, there are tears, and you try to consider what you're going to do. But I knew that I couldn't carry on.'

NOW Currently a podiatrist, treating ailments from dodgy hips to even dodgier feet. The journey to this unusual career began in 1991 when he returned to education at Salford and Manchester universities and gained a Bsc (Hons) in Podiatry. 'I had that many injuries during my career that I got very friendly with Jim McGregor, who was the physio at Manchester United,' recalls Whiteside. 'I was in the medical room so often that I started to ask him about his job, and he would give me the names of muscles to go home and learn.' Today, the Professional Footballers' Association employ Whiteside to help youth team players with minor injuries such as shin splints. It's an important role, and that's why I'm so pleased that the PFA backed me up,' he told *FourFourTwo*. 'So often I see kids with shin splints, 'I'ts by simply putting insoles into their boots I can solve the problem. The clubs that need me are the ones that can't afford to have their own podiatrists, and because I'm employed by the PFA, they receive a free-of-charge service.'

Norman Whiteside
MANCHESTER UNITED

4 LES SEALEY (1957-2001)

Coventry City, Luton Town, Plymouth Argyle (loan), Manchester United, Aston Villa, Coventry City (loan), Birmingham City (loan), Manchester United, Blackpool, West Ham, Leyton Orient, West Ham, Bury (loan) • 1976-2000

BORN 29 September 1957

POSITION Goalkeeper

HONOURS Manchester United: FA Cup Winner 1990; European Cup Winners' Cup Winner 1991

THEN Despite winning the 1990 FA Cup Final replay with Manchester United (a 1-0 victory over Crystal Palace) during a loan spell and forcing the omission of regular United number one Jim Leighton, Les Sealey is probably best remembered for his seven years at Luton Town. The reasons? Reckless charges from goal, madcap behaviour and ludicrous celebrations with the Luton fans. For the most part, however, his knack of burning across the Kenilworth Road 'astroturf' without a wince marked him as an eccentric. Injuries – when they did occur – were treated with a dutiful indifference. Later, during United's clash with Sheffield Wednesday in the 1991 League Cup Final, Sealey's knee was sliced to the bone in a collision. He refused to leave the pitch, played through the pain and fainted after the match. It was later revealed he could have lost his leg. A few weeks on, he faced Barcelona in the 1991 European Cup Winners' Cup Final (a 2-1 victory). There were also spells at Villa (1991-1993), Coventry (1992, loan), West Ham (1994-1996), Birmingham City (1992, loan), Blackpool (1994, loan) and Bury (1998, loan), Sealey played the last of his 550 appearances during his second spell at West Ham (1996-2000) against Manchester United in 1998.

WHAT HAPPENED NEXT? After his retirement, Sealey became a goalkeeping coach at West Ham, working with the trainees, including his two sons Joe and George. On August 19 2001 he suffered a fatal heart attack. 'Les was larger than life,' says former West Ham manager, Harry Redknapp. 'He was such a lovely, enthusiastic character. He was a great goalkeeping coach and he absolutely loved West Ham. He was irreplaceable.' He was 43 years-old.

Les Sealey
MANCHESTER UNITED

5 MARK WARD

Oldham Athletic, West Ham, Manchester City, Everton, Birmingham City, Huddersfield Town, Wigan Athletic • 1983-1996

BORN 10 October 1962

POSITION Winger

HONOURS None

THEN Define the term 'tricksy winger' to a football novice and chances are you'll describe Mark Ward to a tee. All pointy elbows and amusement arcade footwork, Ward was a livewire on the flank, particularly during his spell at West Ham (1985-1989), where he fed the goal-hungry frontline of Tony Cottee and Frank McAvennie. Following a top three finish in 1986, West Ham failed to develop their emerging team and were eventually relegated in 1989. Ward wanted out, moving first to Manchester City for £1 million and then Howard Kendall's Everton for £1.1 million two years later. He scored twice on his debut in a 3-1 win over Arsenal, a game he describes as 'the best of my career'. He later moved to Birmingham as player-coach but failed to hit it off with manager, Barry Fry before short spells at Huddersfield Town (1996) and Wigan (1996).

NOW Detained at Her Majesty's pleasure in 2005 for eight years for possessing cocaine with intent to supply. Ward's troubles began when he returned from a spell in Australia. 'On my return to England, I became severely ill with a suspected aneurysm and had to spend months in hospital,' he told *Observer Sports Monthly*. 'I was skint. That was when someone made me an offer I shouldn't have accepted. They said they'd pay me a weekly wage if I rented a house in my name and handed the keys over to them. I knew something dodgy was going on in the flat, but wasn't sure how dodgy. I never went there. Then the police raided it one day and found £700,000 worth of cocaine. My name was on the rental agreement; I was arrested. I'm hoping to do my time as straightforwardly as possible and get out as soon as I can. I'm keeping fit and trying to write a book about my life.'

Mark Ward
EVERTON

6 JEREMY GOSS

Norwich City, Hearts, Colchester United • 1984-1999

BORN 11 May 1965

POSITION Midfielder

HONOURS None

THEN Jeremy Goss didn't score many goals during his football career (14 in 188 appearances), though his successful strikes often bordered on the spectacular. Mention his name and one image springs to mind: the sight of Goss, picking up a poorly-timed clearance from Germany midfielder Lothar Matthäus as Norwich took on Bayern Munich in the second round, first leg of the 1994 UEFA Cup at the Olympic Stadium. In a flash, he'd volleyed the ball into the back of the net – the icing on Norwich's 3-2 aggregate victory. 'I scored some better ones than that though,' he laughs. This was a career highlight, however. Mainly a one club man, Goss spent 12 years at Carrow Road, with short spells at Hearts (1996-1997) in Scotland and Colchester United (1998-1999) at the close of his career. For the most part he was a fringe player at Norwich, rising through the ranks and spending long spells on the sidelines, though 'Gozza' was fondly noted for his perseverance and curly locks.

NOW The hair has gone but Goss remains linked to Norwich City, working in the sales department in a more traditional nine-to-five environment. 'I was at the youth academy for a while,' he says. 'And then I moved into the sales team. I also own an amusement arcade in Great Yarmouth, but I'm trying to sell that. It's got everything in it – cranes and video games, but I haven't spent ten pence in it. I have no interest in them. I look totally different now – I've lost all my hair and aged considerably. When you're a footballer you're in dreamworld. Then when you come out of the game it changes – I didn't make a fortune, so I had to work and it's a bitter pill to swallow. I don't go on about that Bayern Munich goal either. If people ask me, I'll talk about it, but I don't want be an old player harping on about old times.'

Jeremy Goss
NORWICH CITY

7 MARCO GABBIADINI

York City, Sunderland, Crystal Palace, Derby County, Birmingham City (loan), Oxford United (loan), Panionios (Greece), Stoke City, York City (loan), Darlington, Northampton Town, Hartlepool • 1985-2004

BORN 20 January 1968

POSITION Striker

HONOURS Sunderland: Division Three Champions 1988

THEN The definitive journeyman. 'Marco Goalo's' adventures spanned 19 years and over 750 appearances, comprising 11 clubs, including an excursion to Greek side Panionios. 'I made my debut at 17,' he says. 'I was around for ages. People were even calling me a veteran when I was 28. A lot of fans think I played for hundreds of clubs.' Beginning at York, Gabbiadini moved to Sunderland in 1987 where he formed an impressive partnership with Eric Gates, scoring the winning goal in the Division Two play-off semi-final against Newcastle. He then made a club record £1.8 million move to Crystal Palace in 1991 where he was seen as a replacement for Ian Wright. After only four months he was sold to Derby for £1 million. Once there he became a first team regular until injury impinged on his appearances and the Premiership dream – Derby had just made the top flight. Following a series of loan moves, Gabbiadini moved to Darlington in 1998 before transfers to Northampton (2000-2003) and Hartlepool (2003-2004). Keyhole surgery on his knee forced him into retirement in January 2004.

NOW Gabbiadini runs an award-winning, five star guest house called Bishops in York. 'I'm not the Basil Fawlty type,' he says. 'I'm from the era where I did OK from football but I wasn't a wealthy man, so I had to work in my retirement. The hotel game is demanding and there's pressure, but I like it. I fancied a break from football because I didn't miss many games during my career. I was rarely injured. I think I averaged 40 matches a season, and I never really had a rest through injury. I took my coaching badges, but you see the pressure on managers in the lower leagues, so I didn't fancy that straightaway, but I am thinking about getting back into the game in one way or another.'

Marco Gabbiadini
NORTHAMPTON TOWN

8 DALE GORDON

Norwich City, Glasgow Rangers, West Ham, Peterborough (loan), Millwall (loan), Bournemouth
• 1984-1997

BORN 9 January 1967

POSITION Winger

HONOURS Glasgow Rangers: Premier League Champions 1992, 1993; Scottish Cup Winner 1992; Scottish League Cup Winner 1993

THEN Instantly recognisable with his stylised 'Five Star' haircut and flashing feet, Gordon's incisive running and goal-seeking passes made him a Norwich City favourite. Having emerged from the youth team, he made his debut against Liverpool in August 1984 and made 206 appearances for the Canaries, scoring 31 goals. By 1991 he'd joined the English player drain to Glasgow Rangers for £1.2 million where he helped the Ibrox outfit to a Skol Cup, the Scottish Cup and two League titles. He then returned south to West Ham in 1993, though Gordon was hardly flushed with success in the East End and injuries dogged his career. Following loan spells at Peterborough (1995) and Millwall (1996), Mel Machin took him to Bournemouth (1996-1997) as player-coach. He finally hung up his boots (and trademarked perm) in February 1997.

NOW Following his retirement from playing, Gordon managed non-League Gorleston alongside former team-mate, Robert Fleck. He later worked at Ipswich Town's youth academy. 'I've lost my Kid Creole and the Coconuts look,' he says. 'But I've still got my hair. It's one of the things people remember me for, especially the fans that collected Panini stickers – which were great by the way, because the players were paid £100 every time they took our picture. I currently run the Dale Gordon Soccer Academy in Great Yarmouth, teaching kids, so I keep in shape. But I don't miss playing football for a living, which my mates find really odd. I began to find it frustrating – I lost a couple of yards at West Ham through injury and when I returned I wasn't enjoying the football. I could still play and I still had the speed of thought, but my legs just couldn't take me there anymore.'

Dale Gordon
NORWICH CITY

9 DAVID ROCASTLE (1967-2001)

Arsenal, Leeds United, Manchester City, Chelsea, Norwich City (loan), Hull City (loan), Sabah (Malaysia) • 1984-1999

BORN 2 May 1967

POSITION Midfielder

HONOURS Arsenal: League Cup Winner 1987; Division One Champions 1989, 1991

THEN The Lewisham-raised midfielder with Copacabana feet, 'Rocky' was a stylish player blessed with grace, strength, imagination and flair. Schooled through the Arsenal youth teams, he became the jewel in George Graham's effective side of the late 1980s, winning 14 England caps, the League Cup in 1987 (following a match-winning goal against Spurs in the semi) and two First Division titles (1989 and 1991) before being sold to Howard Wilkinson's Leeds for £2 million in 1992. 'I can remember not having any mementoes from my time at Arsenal,' he said. 'And going into the club shop and spending a lot of money on photographs and little bits and pieces. Then the next minute we were moving to Leeds.' Injury dogged his Elland Road career before a move to Manchester City in 1993. By the start of the 1994/95 season he was at Chelsea where, over four years, his time on the treatment table outweighed his appearances. Later he had trials at Hertha BSC Berlin (Germany) and loan spells at Norwich City (1997) and Hull City (1997). He finished his career with Malaysian side Sabah.

WHAT HAPPENED NEXT? It was announced that Rocky had non-Hodgkin's lymphoma in February 2001. Despite a course of chemotherapy, he died on 31 March 2001 – he was 33. The tributes quickly followed. 'I met David Rocastle when we played in the same district side,' says Arsenal midfield partner, Michael Thomas. 'He was a special talent as a footballer, but more importantly he was a special person. There were no airs and graces with Rocky. He was down to earth, never big-headed and always had time for everyone.' As part of the celebrations surrounding Highbury's final season, Arsenal devised the David Rocastle Day on 1 April 2006. The game, against Villa, began with a minute of applause – a fitting tribute to this most positive of players.

David Rocastle
ARSENAL

10 STEVE OGRIZOVIC

Chesterfield, Liverpool, Shrewsbury Town, Coventry City • 1977-2000

BORN 12 September 1957

POSITION Goalkeeper

HONOURS Coventry City: FA Cup Winner 1987

THEN Throughout much of the 1980s and early 1990s, Oggy was a legend. At Anfield he built his reputation as a fearless shot stopper, though he was blocked from the starting XI by Ray Clemence. At Coventry City, however, he proved an immovable force, making over 600 appearances (a club record), scoring direct from a goal kick against Sheffield Wednesday in 1986 and appearing for the Football League team which played the Rest of the World (featuring Diego Maradona) at Wembley in 1987. His career highlight came in the same year when Coventry dispatched Spurs in the FA Cup Final. But away from football, Oggy was proving equally adept at cricket. 'I was lucky enough to be a part of the Shropshire side that knocked Yorkshire out of the NatWest Trophy,' he says. 'I also played against Somerset for the Minor Counties. I did bowl Viv Richards but it was no-balled. He was courteous enough to admit that he hadn't heard the call and didn't change his shot. That was nice of him.' He retired from football in 2000.

NOW In 2003, Oggy began working at Coventry City as director of the club's youth academy. 'You have different objectives and responsibilities,' he says, 'but it's great. My job is to manage the department, which looks after 140 kids from the age of nine up until the Under-19s level.' Controversially, he became the victim of an internet hoax in 2003 claiming he'd been kidnapped in Kazakhstan. An online petition for his release was even set up, though this was later exposed as a scam when reporters from the *Coventry Evening Telegraph* called Oggy at the training ground. 'I don't know what that was about,' he says. 'Everybody believed it though. It was obviously someone's idea of a joke. Have I ever been to Kazakhstan? You're joking. I can't even spell it.'

Steve Ogrizovic
COVENTRY CITY

11 PAUL PARKER

Fulham, Queens Park Rangers, Manchester United, Derby County, Sheffield United, Fulham, Chelsea
• 1982-1997

BORN 4 April 1964

POSITION Defender

HONOURS Manchester United: League Cup Winner 1992; Premiership Champions 1993, 1994; FA Cup Winner 1994

THEN Think of Paul Parker and what do you see? An England wall positioned around 20 yards from Peter Shilton's goal in the 1990 World Cup semi-final, most probably. West Germany defender Andreas Brehme is striking a free kick as Parker races forward. His shoulder connects with the ball and diverts its path up and over Shilton and into the net. Cue hysterical German celebrations and mullet ruffling. But think harder and you'll probably remember Parker as the versatile QPR defender capable of controlling the hyperactive Adidas Tangos that pinged across Loftus Road's plastic pitch during the 1980s. 'I knew that if that ball bounced over my head and I couldn't catch it, nobody else was going to,' he says. 'It made a big difference to my career.' Following his World Cup heartache, Parker became a right back and was sold to Manchester United for £2 million in 1991, though his Old Trafford career was potholed with injuries during the latter stages. There were one or two medals to crow about though. And if you think back to that World Cup semi-final once more, you'll remember that Parker quickly made amends by setting up Gary Lineker's equaliser before the inevitable, crushing penalty shootout defeat.

NOW Parker moved away from football in 1997. 'When you leave football you blame everyone else apart from yourself,' he says. 'The phone rarely rings and I wanted to avoid the game for a while. I started a vehicle leasing company, then I became involved in a retail security firm. I couldn't keep away though. I got involved in management at Chelmsford City (1999-2003) then Welling United (2003-2005). But I didn't enjoy it as much as I thought I would.' These days he divides his time between media work on MUTV and Setanta Sport.

Paul Parker
MANCHESTER UNITED

12 CYRILLE REGIS

West Bromwich Albion, Coventry City, Aston Villa, Wolverhampton Wanderers, Wycombe Wanderers, Chester City • 1977-1996

BORN 9 February 1958

POSITION Striker

HONOURS Coventry City: FA Cup Winner 1987

THEN Powerful centre forward who kicked down defenders and racial barriers as one of the First Division's first black footballers. Alongside Brendon Batson and Laurie Cunningham, Regis made up the pioneering 'Three Degrees' trio at West Brom under Ron Atkinson in 1977. Upon signing, 'Smokin' Joe' (as he came to be nicknamed) made an immediate impression, scoring twice on his debut in the League Cup in 1977 and then grabbing a goal in his full League debut a few days later. Not bad for a former electrician who began business in the amateur leagues with Hayes. Regis became a sensation at The Hawthorns. But despite his outstanding ability, the England caps were fewer than expected – he made only five international appearances. On his first call-up, Regis received a bullet through the post, attached with the note, 'You'll get one of these through your knees if you step on the Wembley turf.' He battled on regardless, later playing for Coventry between 1984 and 1991, then Villa (1991-1993), Wolves (1993-1994), Wycombe Wanderers (1994-1995) and Chester City (1995-1996) before retiring through injury at the age of 38.

NOW Began his post-playing career as the reserve team coach for West Brom before qualifying as a football agent in 1999. 'It's good fun,' he says. 'Though we're under scrutiny these days, I work with integrity and within the rules of the game. Today, even the poor players earn £10,000 a week, but that doesn't bother me. It's market forces. I loved my time in football. I worked on a building site before playing, so I've always appreciated the game and I've had a contrast in life. What I do miss is the dressing room banter. Nothing's sacred. They'll take the piss over everything from your hair to your todger, but it was always funny.'

Cyrille Regis
WOLVERHAMPTON WANDERERS

13 MICKEY THOMAS

Wrexham, Manchester United, Everton, Brighton & Hove Albion, Stoke City, Chelsea, West Bromwich Albion, Derby County (loan), Wichita Wings (USA), Shrewsbury Town, Leeds United, Stoke City, Wrexham • 1972-1993

BORN 7 July 1954

POSITION Winger/scoundrel

HONOURS Wrexham: Division Three Champions 1978. Chelsea: Division Two Champions 1984

THEN The football bad boy with more clubs than Tiger Woods, Mickey Thomas is remembered for few football achievements. In short, then: his memorable FA Cup goal for Wrexham against Arsenal in 1992, a Third Division title with Wrexham in 1978, and a goal in Wales' 4-1 drubbing of England in 1980. Off the ball there was plenty to talk about, however. While at Chelsea (1984-1985) he remarked to chairman Ken Bates that he wouldn't mind 'giving one' to a passing girl who later turned out to be Bates' daughter-in-law. And when Thomas's glamour model wife became enraged with his boozy womanising, she trashed the marital home. On the pitch, he even shocked the football world and Jimmy Hill. During one game against Ipswich, he seemingly tumbled to the floor, earning a dubious penalty for Manchester United (1978-1981). In a devilish flash, he winked cheekily at the rolling Match of the Day cameras and became a national villain overnight. Ronaldo, eat your heart out.

NOW These days Thomas involves himself in media work, though he was jailed for 18 months in 1993 after passing counterfeit £10 notes.
'I learnt a lot in prison,' he says. 'I created a lot of headlines when I was a player so I thought it would be good to work on the other side for a while. My career was cut short because of jail, but I have no regrets. I'm looking to the future now.' Sadly, Thomas is discovering that some things can never be forgiven. 'Fans always bring up that wink during the televised game against Ipswich,' he says. 'I couldn't believe the fuss at the time – they showed it on TV every week. The thing is, you do that now and nobody bats an eyelid. I always got the headlines.'

Mickey Thomas
WALES

14 GARY GILLESPIE

Falkirk, Coventry City, Liverpool, Celtic, Coventry City • 1977-1997

BORN 5 July 1960

POSITION Defender

HONOURS Liverpool: Division One Champions 1986, 1988, 1990

THEN Such was Gary Gillespie's impact at Falkirk that he was made skipper of the side at 17 – the world's youngest ever first-team captain in football. His progression showed no signs of slowing. After five years at Coventry City (1978-1983), he transferred to Anfield for £325,000, where he became a vital cog in Liverpool's trophy-snatching team of the 1980s. There were League titles, as Gillespie formed an impressive partnership with Alan Hansen. There were Wembley appearances, though he played in only one FA Cup Final – the 1-0 defeat to Wimbledon in 1988 (he missed the 1986 and 1989 finals). And there were goals – Gillespie scored a hat-trick against Birmingham City in 1986. 'I don't know where that came from,' he laughs. 'I was fortunate to have enjoyed a great career though. If you can live your boyhood dream, then you're very lucky.' Elsewhere, there were international games, including a 1990 World Cup appearance against Brazil, but his trophy days were behind him. Following a £925,000 move to Celtic in 1991, he scored on his debut against former club Falkirk as part of three barren years at Parkhead. He finished his career at Coventry in 1997.

NOW Following a coaching stint at Stockport, things went 'pear-shaped' for Gillespie. 'I drifted out of football,' he says. 'And I haven't been back since. I now work for Radio Merseyside and help to arrange corporate golf days – the Former Liverpool Players' Association also organise a few trips. They're supposed to be exhibition matches, but really it's just an excuse to get drunk. I do miss the day-to-day involvement with a team. And when I commentate on the big games it seems weird – there's nothing like playing in the atmosphere of a big match on a nice night, though cast your mind back to a cold winters evening playing for Liverpool reserves against Oldham and that quickly changes.'

Gary Gillespie
LIVERPOOL

15 DAVE BENNETT

Manchester City, Cardiff City, Coventry City, Sheffield Wednesday, Swindon Town, Shrewsbury Town (loan) • 1978-1992

BORN 11 July 1959

POSITION Winger

HONOURS Coventry City: FA Cup Winner 1987

THEN Dave Bennett's career is best defined by two FA Cup Finals. The first was tainted by defeat when Manchester City (1978-1981) lost to Spurs and a Ricky Villa's solo effort in 1981. 'It was the 100th ever FA Cup Final though,' he says. 'So it was still a pretty special game to play in, despite the result.' Bennett's second FA Cup Final appearance was more enjoyable. As a winger in Coventry City's battling side (1983-1989), he secured a Wembley appearance against Spurs in 1987 with impressive performances and important goals (12 all season) and later scored City's first goal in an unexpected 3-2 win. Following moves to Sheffield Wednesday (1989-1990) and Swindon (1990-1992), he was cursed by bad luck. Bennett broke his leg in only his second Swindon appearance. When loaned to Shrewsbury Town in 1991, history repeated itself: during his second match he broke the same leg again. Retired a year later.

NOW Currently splits his time between the book company, Pearson Education, and the anti-racism organisation, Show Racism The Red Card. Bennett believes that while great strides have been made to curb prejudice within the game, black players still experience racism, particularly when applying for coaching positions. 'I have a lot of top level experience in football,' he says. 'Yet nobody will put me on the first rung of the managerial ladder. It's unbelievable – ten per cent of people playing football are black, but that's not reflected within coaching. As a black player in the 1980s you had to be excellent to make it. The same applies to management now. We're just not getting a look in.'

Dave Bennett
COVENTRY CITY

16 LUTHER BLISSETT

Watford, A.C. Milan, Watford, Bournemouth, Watford, West Bromwich Albion (loan), Bury, Mansfield Town (loan) • 1975-1994

BORN 1 February 1958

POSITION Striker

HONOURS Watford: Division Four Champions 1978

THEN Luther Blissett's international career began in a Roy of the Rovers-style goal blitz. After scoring 27 goals in the 1982-83 season with Watford (including four in an 8-0 win over Sunderland), he nabbed a hat-trick during his full England debut – a 9-0 demolition of the mighty Luxembourg. Sadly, Blissett never scored again at international level and the tabloid press cruelly nicknamed him 'Luther Missitt'. Justification of his ability came with Watford's second place finish in the First Division in 1983 and a shock move to Italian giants A.C. Milan (1983-1984). Once abroad, however, Blissett suffered miserably, scoring only five times in 30 League games. After one season, he returned to Vicarage Road and, in all, totalled 415 appearances and 158 goals during his time at the club. His excursions away from Watford included Bournemouth (1988-1991), West Brom (1992-1993) and Bury (1993) before retirement at Mansfield Town in 1994.

NOW Manager at non-League Chesham United. 'I got into coaching in 1996,' he says. 'In 2002 I went to Newport County as coach and then Portsmouth, but the big jobs have always eluded me. I don't know why. You see so many talented black players trying to get into the management side and it doesn't really happen. But you see their white counterparts walk straight into a job without any qualifications.' Elsewhere, Blissett is currently setting up a motor racing team called Windrush Motorsport to race at Le Mans in 2009. 'I've been racing on and off since 1999,' he says. 'Now we want to get a few more black faces in motorsport.' He's also the inspiration for a bizarre anarchist group called The Luther Blissett Project in Italy. 'It's nothing to do with me. They just adopted my name because there were very few black players in Italy when I was there. They're a political group and they release books.'

Luther Blissett
WATFORD

17 IMRE VARADI

Sheffield United, Everton, Newcastle United, Sheffield Wednesday, West Bromwich Albion, Manchester City, Sheffield Wednesday, Leeds United, Luton Town (loan), Oxford United (loan), Rotherham United, Mansfield Town, Scunthorpe United • 1978-1995

BORN 8 July 1959

POSITION Striker

HONOURS None

THEN The Hungarian forward with more house exchanges than the 'Man With A Van' removal service. For much of his career Varadi seemed restless, journeying through football's northern outposts for over 17 years with one or two excursions south(ish) to Oxford (1993) and Luton (1992). At his 12 clubs, fans admired him for the jinking ball skills and turn of pace – particularly at Everton (1979-1981) where he scored the winning goal in a 2-1 win over Liverpool in the FA Cup third round. At Newcastle (1981-1983) he formed profitable partnerships with Kevin Keegan and Chris Waddle before the arrival of Peter Beardsley signalled another visit to the estate agents. After Newcastle, he was sold to Sheffield Wednesday for £285,000. Varadi would prove equally talismanic at Hillsborough, scoring 33 goals in 76 games, but clearly his adventures hadn't ended there and he was off to West Brom (1985-1986), Man City (1986-1988), back to Sheffield Wednesday (1988-1990), Leeds (1990-1993), Luton (a loan, 1992), Oxford (another loan, 1993), Rotherham (1993-1995) before finishing up at Mansfield (1995) and Scunthorpe (1995).

NOW Still a journeyman, Varadi is now a football agent running from ground to ground. 'I've clocked up 25,000 miles in eight months on my new car,' he says. 'I've been an agent for seven years and I look after some good players. I enjoy talking to players, managers and watching the football. It's great fun.' Following his retirement, he dabbled with player-management and joined former team-mate Mel Sterland at Stalybridge as assistant manager before becoming an agent in 2004. 'I've been at quite a few clubs,' he says. 'I get fans coming up to me all the time. The Man City fans still call me Imre Banana. I was a crowd favourite and it gave them an excuse to wave inflatable bananas around.'

Imre Varadi
NEWCASTLE UNITED

18 JOEY JONES

Wrexham, Liverpool, Wrexham, Chelsea, Huddersfield Town, Wrexham • 1973-1992

BORN 4 March 1955

POSITION Defender

HONOURS Wrexham: Welsh Cup Winner 1975. Liverpool: Division One Champions 1977; European Cup Winner 1977. Chelsea: Division Two Champions 1984

THEN Joey Jones loved his three years at Liverpool so much he had 'LFC' tattooed on his arm. The Kop loved him with equal measure. During the 1977 European Cup Final against Borussia Monchengladbach (a 3-1 Reds victory), a banner was passed above the crowd which read, 'Joey ate the frog's legs, made the Swiss roll, now he's munching Gladbach.' Not bad for a stylish defender who only really played for one full season before losing his place to the authoritative Alan Hansen. Jones' tale began at Wrexham, where a successful apprenticeship and an even more successful run in the side – which included an FA Cup quarter-final in 1974 and a Welsh Cup win in 1975 – drew the attentions of Anfield. He signed for £110,000 in July 1975, and spent much of his first year in the reserves. A season later, he'd claimed a first team spot, made his Welsh debut (for a while Jones held the record number of 72 caps) and scooped a League and European Cup double in 1977. Wrexham paid £210,000 for his return in 1978 (a combination of Hansen and Tommy Smith meant future appearances were few and far between), before he moved to Chelsea in 1982. Jones later saw out his career at Huddersfield (1985-1987) and Wrexham again (1987-1992).

NOW Currently coaching at Wrexham. 'I played in the reserves until I was 44,' he says. 'I was also writing up the match reports for the official programme without telling the other players – I was giving myself Man of the Match every week! They couldn't work it out.' At the age of 47, Jones had major heart surgery. 'I remember coming round after the operation. The first people I saw were my wife and (former Chelsea team-mate) Mickey Thomas. Even though I was under the anaesthetic, I heard him say, "Couldn't they have done something with his face in surgery? He's still an ugly bastard."'

Joey Jones
WREXHAM

19 OSSIE ARDILES

Instituto Atletico Central Cordoba (Argentina), Club Atletico Belgrano (Argentina), Huracan (Argentina), Tottenham Hotspur, Paris Saint Germain (France, loan), Blackburn Rovers (loan), Queens Park Rangers, Swindon Town • 1973-1990

BORN 3 August 1952

POSITION Midfielder/Wembley hero

HONOURS Tottenham Hotspur: FA Cup Winner 1981; UEFA Cup Winner 1984

THEN Few footballers have their name immortalised on vinyl. But when Ossie guided Spurs to the 1981 FA Cup Final against Manchester City, one rhyming couplet from Chas & Dave's accompanying single 'Ossie's Dream' propelled the diminutive Argentinean onto national radio: 'Ossie's going to Wembley, his knees have gone all trembly.' His cultural impact was more far-reaching. As the more consistent of Spurs' two South American signings of 1978 (the other being Ricky Villa), Ardiles kick-started a foreign revolution that began with a ticker tape parade at White Hart Lane and still gathers pace today. Nevertheless, at their time of signing (after Argentina's World Cup victory), the duo were considered incredibly exotic. He was a nifty player, too, linking well in a midfield featuring Glenn Hoddle among others. His creative play later turned Spurs into cup kings and a European tour de force. The Falklands War tempered his progress and after a loan spell at Paris Saint Germain in 1982, Ardiles returned to Spurs before continuing his career at Blackburn on loan (1988), QPR (1988-1989) and Swindon Town (1989-1990).

NOW Following coaching stints which included Swindon Town (1989-1991), Newcastle (1991-1992), West Brom (1992-1993), Spurs (1993-1994) and Japanese team Shimizu S-Pulse (1996-1998), Ossie took over at Israeli team Beitar Jerusalem FC for the 2006/07 season, though he was sacked after a couple of months following poor results. 'Playing for Spurs in the 1981 FA Cup Final was one of the highlights of my career,' he says. 'We played a very attractive, South American-style of football. Diego Maradona also played at my testimonial at White Hart Lane in 1986. There was talk (of him signing for Spurs), but nothing came of it.' Became manager of Argentinian side Hurucan in September 2007.

Ossie Ardiles
TOTTENHAM HOTSPUR

20 GLENN COCKERILL

Lincoln City, Swindon Town, Lincoln City, Sheffield United, Southampton, Leyton Orient, Fulham, Brentford • 1975-1998

BORN 25 August 1959

POSITION Midfielder

HONOURS None

THEN Midfield playmaker with a pile-driving shot, Cockerill is occasionally remembered for his time at Southampton, despite attaining near journeyman status after spells with Lincoln City (twice), Swindon and Sheffield United. For the most part, however, he is recalled for a bout of fisticuffs with Arsenal midfielder Paul Davis in 1988. In fairness, fisticuffs is somewhat untrue – it suggests the duo were embroiled in a fight. The reality? Davis 'brained' Cockerill on the blindside, sending him to the floor. After being carried off the field, Cockerill was treated for a broken jaw, an incident which overshadowed an otherwise impressive career. At The Dell, he made his name as a creative midfielder, earning the club's Player of the Season award in the mid-1980s. He later moved to London at Leyton Orient (1993-1996) and Fulham (1996-1997), before a final year at Brentford, though this happened two years after Davis – another ex-Bee – had left the club.

NOW Was manager of Conference club Woking until March 2007. 'I was a few months short of my 39th birthday when I retired from playing,' he says. 'I wanted to play for as long as possible, and getting into coaching was the next best thing. The long, curly hair went and I had spells at Fulham, Palace and Woking. I was known to give players the hairdryer treatment once in a while – 80 per cent of a manager's job is about man-management, so you have to know how to treat players. Have I seen Paul Davis since the incident? Oh yeah, I kicked him in the Masters tournament once, so I got my own back. It was one of the first incidents where video evidence was used – that's why it made all the headlines.'

Glenn Cockerill
SOUTHAMPTON

21 JUSTIN FASHANU (1961-1998)

Norwich City, Nottingham Forest, Southampton (loan), Notts County, Brighton & Hove Albion, Manchester City, West Ham, Leyton Orient, Torquay (player-coach), Airdrie, Hearts
• 1978-1994

BORN 19 February 1961

POSITION Striker

HONOURS None

THEN A headline machine, Fashanu first bulldozed his way into the First Division with a powerful build that scattered defenders like empty beer cans. A rocket shot against Liverpool at Carrow Road in 1980 made him a household name – a dipping volley from 30 yards, it became a fixture on the 101 Great Goals video compilations. Fashanu would later become English football's first £1 million black player when he signed for Nottingham Forest, but the good times ended there. A closeted gay, Fashanu crossed swords with Forest gaffer Brian Clough, recorded an unreleased pop single, revealed his sexuality to the public in 1990, tried to become a monk, titillated the tabloids during his friendship with Coronation Street's Julie Goodyear and accrued huge debts before quitting English football in 1992. 'He lived the life of the modern professional footballer long before it was accepted,' says his manager at Notts County, Howard Wilkinson.

WHAT HAPPENED NEXT: Fashanu was found hanged in a lock-up garage in London in May 1998, having been on the run from police in Maryland, USA following a coaching stint with A-League team, Maryland Mania. A teenage boy had accused him of sexual assault at a party. He returned to England immediately, but was found dead weeks later. 'Well, if anyone finds this note hopefully I won't be around to see it,' he wrote in his suicide letter. 'Being gay and a personality is so hard, but everybody has it hard at the moment, so I can't complain about that ... But I tried my best. This seems to be a really hard world.' He was 37 years-old.

Justin Fashanu
NORWICH CITY

22 DANNY WALLACE

Southampton, Manchester United, Millwall (loan), Birmingham City, Wycombe Wanderers (loan)
• 1980-1995

BORN 21 January 1964

POSITION Striker

HONOURS Manchester United: FA Cup Winner 1990

THEN A pocket-sized powerhouse (he stood at only 5ft 5in) and part of the Wallace brothers trio (the others being Rod and Ray), Danny banged in spectacular goals for fun. During the first live televised game at The Dell in 1984, the then Southampton forward scored an overhead kick and a diving header past Liverpool keeper Bruce Grobbelaar. His first strike later scooped the Goal of the Season award. With over 300 first-team games at Southampton, Wallace's explosive pace attracted the attentions of Manchester United. He was sold for £1.2 million in 1989, and his return was almost immediate. In 1990, Wallace helped United to the FA Cup – Alex Ferguson's first English trophy. Following a string of injuries and a loss of form, he moved first to Birmingham City (1993) and then Wycombe Wanderers (1995) before leaving the game that same year.

NOW During retirement, the reasons behind Wallace's injury struggles became clear – he was diagnosed with Multiple Sclerosis in 1996. 'It was a real shock,' he says. 'I went into depression for five years. I wasn't working or going out – I would just stay indoors. But it was also a relief (to be diagnosed), because I realised why I was struggling with injuries so much. By 2000, I pulled myself out of it. I've since been working quite actively to increase awareness of the disease – I started The Danny Wallace Foundation in 2005 and I did the London Marathon in 2006 to raise money. I walked it in five and a half days. Not being able to run, I felt it was an amazing achievement. I have spinal MS – so I can be good on one day, I can be bad on another. I just have to take it as it comes.'

Danny Wallace
MANCHESTER UNITED

23 PHIL NEAL

Northampton Town, Liverpool, Bolton Wanderers • 1968-1989

BORN 29 February 1951

POSITION Right back

HONOURS Liverpool: Division One Champions 1976, 1977, 1979, 1980, 1982, 1983, 1984, 1986; European Cup Winner 1977, 1978, 1981, 1984; UEFA Cup Winner 1976; League Cup Winner 1981, 1982, 1983, 1984

THEN The only player to come close to matching Roy Race's incredible trophy haul. Neal was a medal collector, picking up 23 winner's badges in all competitions (including Charity Shields and European Super Cups) with Liverpool while making 455 League appearances and scoring 41 goals between 1974 and 1985. More impressively, he was the only player to appear in Liverpool's first five European Cup Finals. A cool customer on the penalty spot (he scored the spot kick in the 1977 European Cup Final against Borussia Monchengladbach) and an ever present for long spells (he played 365 consecutive matches between 1975 and 1983), Neal also made headway on the international scene, notching up 50 England appearances between 1976 and 1983. Later moved to Bolton as player-manager in 1985 before retiring in 1989.

NOW Following his managerial stint at Bolton (1985-1992), he took charge at Coventry City (1993-1995) and Manchester City (1996). Neal's most memorable post, though, was as right-hand man to England gaffer Graham Taylor. His job came under scrutiny in Channel 4 'car crash' documentary, An Impossible Job. 'I was working on a match-to-match basis with Graham while I was at Coventry,' he says. 'I've said it before, the Channel 4 documentary didn't do me any good whatsoever. I've since seen the light and got out of management. I'm a media man now and I do after dinner stuff too. But I've also taken up skiing, so I'm doing things I really enjoy now. I had a new hip put in recently, I'm looking forward to testing it out.'

Phil Neal
LIVERPOOL

24 ARTHUR ALBISTON

Manchester United, West Bromwich Albion, Dundee, Chesterfield (loan), Chester City, Molde (Norway) • 1974–1992

BORN 14 July 1957

POSITION Left back

HONOURS Manchester United: FA Cup Winner 1977, 1983, 1985

THEN An ever-reliable full back, Albiston was brought through the Manchester United youth ranks, before stamping his authority on the first-team. He made his debut against Man City in 1974 and left the club 14 years later. 'You can't beat playing football at Old Trafford in front of 60,000 fans,' he says. He joined former United gaffer, Big Ron Atkinson at West Bromwich Albion in 1988, but didn't last long in the Midlands. A season later he was in Scotland at Dundee, before moving on a loan deal to Chesterfield (1990), Chester City (1991) and Norwegian side Molde (1992). Thankfully, he was familiar with international excursions – Albiston made 14 Scottish appearances, including a game in the 1986 World Cup against Uruguay.

NOW Works as a presenter on Manchester United's TV channel, MUTV. 'I had a spell coaching the United Under-15s from 1995 to 2001,' he says. 'But I started working on the local BBC radio station for ten years and then I started working for MUTV. I just stumbled into it really. It's a nice way to keep involved in the game. I really enjoy it. All ex-footballers are big kids at heart, so watching the game is the next best thing to playing. Because I have an understanding of how the game works and how the players feel, I get on with the team. And I've never been on the end of a Fergie hairdryer.'

Arthur Albiston
MANCHESTER UNITED

25 CLAYTON BLACKMORE

Manchester United, Middlesbrough, Bristol City (loan), Barnsley, Notts County, Bangor City
• 1982-2006

BORN 23 September 1964

POSITION Defender/midfielder

HONOURS Manchester United: FA Cup Winner 1990, European Cup Winners' Cup Winner 1991; League Cup Winner 1992; Premier League Champions 1993

THEN Versatile defender who played in all first-team shirts from two to 11 ('plus some other numbers when I was stuck on the bench'). Blackmore first came through the United youth system and was equally adept in defence and across the park in midfield. In total he spent 20 years at the club, having joined as a schoolboy. His Old Trafford career was sprinkled with winners' medals and 39 international caps for Wales too, but after dropping out of first team contention, he moved to Middlesbrough in 1994. He saw out his career at Bristol City (1996, loan), Barnsley (1999), Notts County (1999-2000) and Bangor City (2001-2006) in the League of Wales, where he used the European experience gleaned at United in the UEFA and Intertoto Cup competitions. 'People just kept asking me to play a game,' he laughs. 'So I did.'

NOW Divides his time between playing for Welsh side, Porthmadog and working in the recruitment industry. 'My friend runs his own company,' he says. 'So I'll work for him sometimes. We help employ fruit and veg pickers for Sainsbury's. It's nice to get your hands dirty. I was mollycoddled at United, so it's good to live in the real world. I'll also work on the commercial side at (United TV Station) MUTV. And I sometimes go away with the former United players for exhibitions in Dubai, which is always nice. I get recognised more now than when I was actually playing – we're on the TV more these days. And people are always coming up to me with old sticker books to sign.'

Clayton Blackmore
MANCHESTER UNITED

26 VIV ANDERSON

Nottingham Forest, Arsenal, Manchester United, Sheffield Wednesday, Barnsley, Middlesbrough
• 1974-1995

BORN 29 July 1956

POSITION Right back

HONOURS Nottingham Forest: Division One Champions 1978; League Cup Winner 1978, European Cup Winner 1979, 1980. Arsenal: League Cup Winner 1987

THEN An international and club legend, Anderson was the first black player to represent England at full international level (West Brom's Laurie Cunningham had already played for the England Under-21s) when he made his debut in a friendly against Czechoslovakia at Wembley in 1978. He also scooped major honours with Nottingham Forest (1974-1984) in Europe and played top flight football with Arsenal (1984-1987) and Man United (1987-1990). Despite his pace and leggy, ball-winning tackles, Anderson would spend much of his international career playing second fiddle to Phil Neal, Mick Mills (in the 1982 World Cup) and Gary Stevens. He even travelled with two World Cup squads (1982 and 1986) without making it onto the pitch. Moved to Sheffield Wednesday (1990-1993) where he enjoyed a Wembley swansong, reaching the League and FA Cup Finals in 1993, but losing both to Arsenal. Saw out his career as Barnsley player-manager (1993-1994) and a player-coach at Middlesbrough (1994-1995).

NOW Works with a hospitality company called Northwest Events. 'We get people over to Old Trafford on Matchdays and organise golf events. I also run a football academy in Dubai with my former team-mate, Tony Woodcock. A lot of clubs have gone there in pre-season, but they haven't had the facilities to train before, so we provide them. I'd never say never to never management, but there's so much other stuff going on.' Anderson was also recently placed in the English Football Hall of Fame. 'I paid a lot of money for that,' he laughs. 'I still get recognised when I come down to London, but only by the cabbies.'

Viv Anderson
ENGLAND

27 LAURIE CUNNINGHAM (1956-1989)

Leyton Orient, West Bromwich Albion, Real Madrid (Spain), Manchester United (loan), Sporting de Gijon (Spain), Olympique Marseille (France), Leicester City, Rayo Vallecano (Spain), Charleroi (Belgium), Wimbledon, Rayo Vallecano (Spain) • 1974-1989

BORN 8 March 1956

POSITION Winger

HONOURS Real Madrid: La Liga Champion 1980; Spanish Copa del Rey 1980, 1982. Wimbledon: FA Cup Winner 1988

THEN Swashbuckling winger who, alongside Brendon Batson and Cyrille Regis, made up the trio of players who broke into manager Ron Atkinson's West Brom side. Cunningham was soon called up to the England Under-21 team for a friendly against Scotland in April 1977, making him the first black player to receive England recognition at any level. He scored on his debut and later earned a full cap against Wales in May 1979 – the first appearance of a black player in a competitive fixture. Interest in Cunningham was at a premium and he was soon sold to Real Madrid in 1979, where he was nicknamed Black Flash, though he never recreated his goal-scoring exploits of previous seasons, despite helping Madrid to a Spanish League and Cup double in 1980, and a European Cup Final appearance in 1981. After four years he was loaned to Man United (1983), later moving to Sporting de Gijon (1983-1984), Marseille (1984-1985), Leicester (1985-1986), Rayo Vallecano (1986-1987 and 1988-1989) and Charleroi (1987), before winning an FA Cup winner's medal with Wimbledon in 1988.

WHAT HAPPENED NEXT? Having secured promotion to the Spanish top flight during his second spell at Rayo Vallecano, Cunningham was killed in a car crash just outside Madrid in 1989 when his car careered into a tree. He was 33 years-old. Strangely, his death went largely unreported in Britain, but the impact within football was writ large. 'We were like two peas in a pod for two years,' says Cyrille Regis. 'We made a big difference to the black kids in this country. We cleared a path for those who came after us.'

Laurie Cunningham
WEST BROM

28 MIKE 'MICKY' HAZARD

Tottenham Hotspur, Chelsea, Portsmouth, Swindon Town, Tottenham Hotspur • 1978-1995

BORN 5 February 1960

POSITION Midfielder

HONOURS Tottenham Hotspur: FA Cup Winner 1982; UEFA Cup Winner 1984. Swindon: First Division Play-off Winner 1993

THEN According to the 1982 FA Cup Final programme, bubble-haired midfielder Mike Hazard was: 'a teetotaller whose celebration drink is blackcurrant and lemonade, this Sunderland-born attacking midfielder has soared from stand-in to star this season. Drafted in last October as a replacement for injured (Ricky) Villa, he staked his claim with some fine and usually important goals and has recently been given the Ardiles role.' Not bad for starters, but by 1984, Hazard was an FA Cup and UEFA Cup winner with Spurs. He later moved to Chelsea for five years (1985-1990) and Portsmouth (1990) before being snapped up by former Spurs team-mate and Swindon manager Ossie Ardiles for £130,000 in 1990. Hazard became a major figure, helping the club to play-off success in 1993 and securing Premiership promotion. He played out his career in the top flight, though this was done with a £50,000 return to White Hart Lane in 1993. Retired from the game in 1995.

NOW A London cabbie, though Hazard has spent time in coaching, first with Spurs and then Palace until 2007. 'It's funny,' he says. 'I've played in FA Cup and UEFA Cup Finals in the biggest stadiums against the best players in the world, but nothing gets the blood pressure going like the traffic lights in London. I like cabbing but I find it very demanding because being in traffic all day is very stressful. I've worked outdoors all my life, so it's very different. But I'm my own boss, I go out to work when I want, I come home when I want and I'm free to make my own decisions. People do recognise me though. I picked up a couple outside Stamford Bridge a while back and after 20 minutes it dawned on them who I was. I had to get out, hug them and pose for photos.'

Mike 'Micky' Hazard
CHELSEA

29 TREVOR STEVEN

Burnley, Everton, Glasgow Rangers, Olympique Marseille (France), Glasgow Rangers • 1980-1997

BORN 21 September 1963

POSITION Midfielder

HONOURS Everton: FA Cup Winner 1984; Division One Champions 1985, 1987; European Cup Winners' Cup Winner 1985. Glasgow Rangers: Scottish Premier League Champions 1990, 1992, 1993, 1994. Olympique Marseille: French Division One Champions 1991

THEN Compared to the flashing feet of Chris Waddle and John Barnes on the England flanks, Everton's Trevor Steven cut a distinctly ordinary figure. Manager Bobby Robson was renowned for preferring the simple approach, however, and Steven ousted Chris Waddle on the right wing for England's 3-0 win over Poland in the final group game of the 1986 World Cup. Robson's choice was justified: Steven orchestrated two goals for free-scoring striker, Gary Lineker. Despite his no-nonsense approach, Steven was not without flair. Swerving crosses and incisive through balls were his forte. During his time at Everton (1983-1989) Steven built a profitable partnership with right back Gary Stevens (before his move to Rangers) and an equally robust trophy haul – two League titles, an FA Cup win and a European Cup Winners' Cup were scooped by Howard Kendall's men before the post-Heysel ban on English clubs in Europe. It was for this reason that many English players moved to Rangers in the early 1990s, where European football was on offer. Steven spent two equally profitable spells at Ibrox (with a one year, £5.5 million move to France in 1991 in between) where his partnership with Gary Stevens was rekindled in 1989-1991 and 1992. Retired in 1997.

NOW Following his retirement, Steven became involved in the media, working with both the BBC and Irish broadcasting channel RTE. He also works as a football agent, representing several Rangers and Celtic players and has opened a shop specialising in children's footwear in Glasgow's city centre called Famous Feet.

Trevor Steven
ENGLAND

30 BRYAN GUNN

Aberdeen, Norwich City, Hibernian • 1980-1999

BORN 22 December 1963

POSITION Goalkeeper

HONOURS Aberdeen: European Cup Winners' Cup Winner 1983; Scottish Cup Winner 1983

THEN The crowd-charming goalkeeper who won cult status with a string of gravity-defying performances and a gritty attitude in the Norwich goal and a gritty attitude. In the early 1990s, when Gunn's daughter Francesca was diagnosed with leukaemia, he shaved his head in support and received rapturous applause from supporters. When she died in 1992, Gunn bravely played for Norwich against QPR just days afterwards. Within the 477 appearances he made for Norwich between 1986 and 1998, Gunn was an immovable force. He was twice voted Norwich City Player of the Year (1986 and 1988), and helped the Canaries to their highest League finish (third place in the Premiership) in 1993. Sadly his only silverware, came at Pittodrie (1980-1986) where he picked up a Scottish Cup and European Cup Winners' Cup medal with Aberdeen despite being an unused substitute. Also claimed six international caps with Scotland.

NOW Following retirement, Gunn took up employment in the Norwich City hospitality department. In 2006 he released his autobiography *In Where It Hurts* and a year later was promoted to Club Liaison Officer at Carrow Road – Gunn currently handles all team transfers. Bizarrely in 2002, he was made Sheriff of Norwich by the City Council for one year. He ranks his funniest moment in football as a pre-match bust-up between Norwich City striker Chris Sutton and kit man Jock Robertson before the UEFA Cup tie with Bayern Munich in 1993. 'All because Chris knocked over a pile of towels. Jock was very proud of his dressing room.' Currently dealing with the aches and pains of a former professional keeper: 'An arthritic problem with my back plus the usual aches and pains after two broken legs, a dislocated ankle, a broken cheekbone, broken hand, double hernia operation and a dislocated collarbone.'

Bryan Gunn
NORWICH CITY.

31 TERRY GIBSON

Tottenham Hotspur, Coventry City, Manchester United, Wimbledon, Swindon Town (loan), Peterborough United, Barnet • 1979-1995

BORN 23 December 1962

POSITION Striker

HONOURS Wimbledon: FA Cup Winner 1988

THEN Despite playing for the glamour sides of Tottenham Hotspur and Manchester United, Terry Gibson's greatest success came as part of Wimbledon's Crazy Gang team when he helped overturn Liverpool in the FA Cup Final in 1988. Typically, the game was preceded by chaos. Half the Wimbledon team were drunk the night before, and Gibson slept in his football boots – he'd secured a lucrative sponsorship deal and was softening the leather for the following day. Gibson started as an apprentice at White Hart Lane where he served as a peripheral figure. A move to Coventry in 1983 increased his appearances and goals (43 in 98 League appearances), though following his move to Old Trafford in 1986 he spent long spells on the sidelines, only contributing one goal. High spirits followed at Wimbledon before career closing spells at Peterborough (1993) and Barnet (1993-1995). Retired in 1995.

NOW Gibson was appointed to the coaching staff at Fulham in 2007. Following his retirement from playing, he worked at Barnet and later kept himself busy commercially – he became involved in a Beach Head Tennis Masters event in the Costa Del Sol in 2005, ran a company producing football club bicycles and 'worked on property' in Spain where his wife was a florist. Today, the hair is all gone. 'I've got a bad back, bad knees, bad groin, bad hips and bad ankles,' he says. 'Apart from that I'm fine.'

Terry Gibson
WIMBLEDON

32 PAT JENNINGS

Watford, Tottenham Hotspur, Arsenal, Tottenham Hotspur • 1963-1985

BORN 12 June 1945

POSITION Goalkeeper

HONOURS Tottenham Hotspur: FA Cup Winner 1967; UEFA Cup Winner 1972; League Cup winner 1971, 1973 (CAP Winner). Arsenal: FA Cup Winner 1979

THEN Colossal-fisted goalkeeper who played for both Arsenal (1977-1985) and Spurs (1964-1977) long before the Sol Campbell controversy. 'The derby games were the only games I hated because I never had bad feelings for Tottenham fans, but obviously wanted to win,' he says. Jennings was a reliable shot stopper who regularly makes the fantasy XIs of Spurs fans of all generations, and is remembered for his goal-scoring adventure against Manchester United in the 1967 Charity Shield. 'There was a free kick on the edge of our area,' he says. 'I launched it and was hoping to hit Alan Gilzean upfront. Gilly missed it. (United keeper) Alex Stepney had come out and it bounced over his head and went in the back of the net. I was stunned.' Other notable Jennings trivia: he played over 1,000 club games and retired from international football with Northern Ireland in the 1986 World Cup finals at the age of 41. His last appearance was against Brazil. Given that he'd made his international debut in the same game as George Best in 1964 against Wales, this makes Jennings' consistency and longevity unquestionable.

NOW Goalkeeping coach at Spurs where he's worked since 1993. 'I was a neighbour of Ossie Ardiles,' he told *Hotspur* magazine. 'When he was manager, everyone was employing goalkeeping coaches so he invited me down one day a week to look after Big Erik (Thorstvedt) and (Ian) Walker. The boys enjoyed it so much that Big Erik asked whether I could come in two days a week instead and I ended up pretty much full-time under (former Spurs manager, Christian) Gross. But I couldn't carry that on because of outside pressures, so I do one or two days a week now. I'm usually entertaining in the Spurs Legends Lounge for home games and it's good to be able to discuss matches afterwards with the goalkeepers.'

Pat Jennings
ARSENAL

33 TOMMY CATON (1962-1993)

Manchester City, Arsenal, Oxford United, Charlton Athletic • 1979-1993

BORN 6 October 1962

POSITION Central defender

HONOURS None

THEN Cauliflower-haired centre back with a fearsome shot. Caton was once reported to have fired a training session ball so hard that it burst through the reinforced wire protecting a clubhouse window, shattering the glass behind. Also effective in defence: Caton captained England schoolboys before making his Manchester City debut at the age of 16. From then on, his career moved at lightning pace. At 18, Caton had appeared in an FA Cup Final (1981, City v Spurs). By 1982 he'd played 100 First Division games – the youngest player to achieve this feat at 19 years and five months of age. And in 1983, he was sold to Arsenal for £500,000. After two years at Highbury, the ascendant Tony Adams and Martin Keown had pinched his place and Caton was on his way out. In 1987 he was sold to Oxford United and named club captain. Following their relegation in 1988, Caton was sold to Charlton where an injury-ravaged spell forced his retirement in 1993.

WHAT HAPPENDED NEXT? A month after his retirement from professional football, Caton died of a heart attack on Friday, 30 April 1993. He was only 30 years-old. His son Andrew currently plays for Swindon Town.

Tommy Caton
ARSENAL

34 TONY PARKS

Tottenham Hotspur, Oxford United (loan), Gillingham (loan), Brentford, Queens Park Rangers (loan), Fulham, West Ham, Stoke City, Falkirk, Blackpool, Burnley, Doncaster Rovers, Scarborough, Halifax Town • 1980-2002

BORN 16 January 1963

POSITION Goalkeeper

HONOURS Tottenham Hotspur: UEFA Cup Winner 1984

THEN Tony Parks appeared in relatively few first-team matches in his career, which is weird given that he played for 14 teams over a 22 year period. Of the total 264 games featuring Parks, one sticks in the memory: Spurs' victorious UEFA Cup Final victory over Anderlecht in 1984. In the second leg at White Hart Lane, with the game poised at 1-1, Parks became a penalty shootout hero, winning the game with two saves. Following his goal-line heroics, he was afforded superstar status and was even invited onto the TV:AM sofa, though the celebrations had taken their toll and Parks had lost his voice in the early hours of the morning. '(Presenter) Anne Diamond looked at me as if to say, "bloody footballers"', he says. From then on, Parks struggled to match those European heights. He was farmed out on loan before clocking up the miles between the sticks of Brentford, QPR, Fulham, West Ham, Stoke, Falkirk, Blackpool, Burnley, Donny Rovers, Scarborough and Halifax. Retired in 2002.

NOW Parks works as one of the FA's goalkeeping coaches alongside former Spurs team-mate, Ray Clemence. The UEFA Cup remains his career highlight. 'With hindsight, maybe it was a case of too much too soon,' he says. 'Perhaps I thought it was going to be like that every year. I would have loved to have had that experience every season, but if it was only to come once I think I would have been able to appreciate it more if it had come later in my career. Saying that, it's not a bad thing to be remembered for!'

Tony Parks
TOTTENHAM HOTSPUR

35 ALAN TAYLOR

Rochdale, West Ham, Norwich City, Cambridge United, Vancouver Whitecaps (Canada), Hull City, Burnley, Bury, Norwich City • 1973-1989

BORN 14 November 1953

POSITION Striker

HONOURS West Ham: FA Cup Winner 1975

THEN The FA Cup made a hero of Alan Taylor in 1975. Having been rejected by Preston North End as a youngster, he moved into non-League football with Morecambe before being snapped up by Rochdale and later John Lyall's West Ham. Having signed at Upton Park in November 1974, he was injury stricken for two months before making his debut in the FA Cup quarter-finals against Arsenal at Highbury. Taylor – then 21 – scored in both halves before hitting a double in both the semis (against Ipswich) and the Wembley Final (against Bobby Moore's Fulham). Cue cult status in London's East End. 'What a moment,' he says. 'All the West Ham fans going mad. I don't mind admitting it brought a lump to my throat.' Following the Hammers' European Cup Winners' Cup Final defeat against Anderlecht the following season, injuries once again sidelined Taylor. West Ham were relegated in 1978 and he moved to Norwich a year later, before spells at Cambridge, Hull, Burnley, Bury and Vancouver Whitecaps, though nothing could match his explosive FA Cup adventure of 1975.

NOW Following his retirement in 1989, Taylor became a milkman. He also had spells in amateur football in East Anglia with Thetford Town and Dereham. Now operates a newsagent in Norwich with his wife Jeanette. According to *FourFourTwo* magazine, his shop is 'heralded as the tidiest in England'.

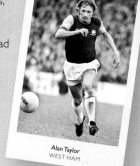

Alan Taylor
WEST HAM

36 KEITH HOUCHEN

Hartlepool United, Leyton Orient, York City, Scunthorpe United, Coventry City, Hibernian, Port Vale, Hartlepool United • 1978-1996

BORN 25 July 1960

POSITION Striker

HONOURS York City: Division Four Champions 1984. Coventry City: FA Cup Winner 1987

THEN Alongside Ricky Villa's twisting dribble and Alan Sunderland's open-mouthed celebrations, Keith Houchen is forever marked as an FA Cup goal-scoring sensation. With the 1987 Final between Spurs and Coventry tipped 2-1 in the Londoners' favour, winger Dave Bennett fired a deep cross into the Tottenham box. Performing a gravity-defying dive, Houchen headed the ball past keeper Ray Clemence and kick-started one of the greatest upsets in memory – Coventry went on to win 3-2. His strike was later voted Match of the Day's 'Goal of the Season'. This was just reward for a hard-working striker. Houchen had clocked up 300 appearances for Hartlepool, Orient, York City and Scunthorpe before his move to Highfield Road in 1986. His giant-killing credentials already apparent, however. In 1985, he scored the only goal in York's historic FA Cup, fourth round win over Arsenal. Houchen later moved to Hibernian in 1989, where the transfer allowed him to play UEFA Cup football, before moves to Port Vale and a spell as player-manager with first club, Hartlepool.

NOW Sacked from management in 1996. Houchen now lets property on Teesside as well as working at Middlesbrough's youth academy. The FA Cup Final victory sticks in the mind as Houchen's career highlight, however. 'Even the mayor of Coventry went crazy,' he says of the celebrations. 'Everyone was out of it by 2am. Policemen were coming in and filling their helmets with champagne. People were chucking the Cup around the room, bouncing it off the walls. At one point someone realised that the lid was missing. Someone was sitting on it. It was all bent out of shape.'

Keith Houchen
HIBERNIAN

37 ROD WALLACE

Southampton, Leeds United, Glasgow Rangers, Bolton Wanderers, Gillingham • 1988-2004

BORN 2 October 1969

POSITION Striker/winger

HONOURS Leeds United: Division One Champions 1992. Glasgow Rangers: Scottish Premier League Champions 1999, 2000; Scottish Cup Winner 1999, 2000; Scottish League Cup Winner 1998

THEN When Rodney Seymour Wallace shouldered brothers Danny and Ray in Southampton's League game against Sheffield Wednesday on 22 October 1988, he made football history. This was the first time three siblings had played alongside one another in English top-flight football. Though initially ignored within Danny's impressive shadow, Rodney soon moved to Leeds in 1991 for £1.6 million (following 45 goals in 128 Southampton games) where he helped Howard Wilkinson's side to a First Division title. He also nabbed a Goal of the Season award following a mazy dribble and long range shot that bamboozled Spurs in 1993/94. Glasgow Rangers came knocking in 1998 and Wallace was soon on the trophy haul, picking up Scottish Cup wins and League titles, before disappointing spells at Bolton (2001-2002) and Gillingham (2002-2004), where injury problems signalled the end of his career.

NOW 'I left Gillingham in 2004,' says Wallace. 'And I finished playing football and just concentrated on renovating my house. I'm looking to get into property development later on, but I'm not working properly at the moment. My wife runs a clothing shop called U R Kidding in Ewell, which specialises in kiddies' clothes, so I help her out with that too. I keep in touch with football – I can now play in the Masters competition and I recently represented the Rangers side in a tournament in Dubai. It's always nice to catch up with the old faces.'

Rod Wallace
GLASGOW RANGERS

38 PAUL MARINER

Plymouth Argyle, Ipswich Town, Arsenal, Portsmouth, Naxxar Lions (Malta) • 1973-1987

BORN 22 May 1953

POSITION Striker

HONOURS Ipswich Town: FA Cup Winner 1978; UEFA Cup Winner 1981

THEN A good old-fashioned number nine, Mariner was a physical force in Bobby Robson's swaggering Ipswich Town team of the late 1970s and 1980s. Marking his talent at Plymouth (1973-1976), Mariner was whisked away to Portman Road for £220,000 where he played vital roles in Ipswich's FA Cup triumph over Arsenal in 1978 (he was Man of the Match) and the 1981 UEFA Cup Final victory over AZ 67 Alkmaar (Mariner scored in the first leg). He was proving an equally effective international figure, making appearances under Ron Greenwood and Bobby Robson, and joining the squads for the 1980 European Championships and the 1982 World Cup Finals where he is best remembered for dragging a distraught Kevin Keegan to his feet following Mighty Mouse's fluffed header in front of an open goal during England's vital second round group game against Spain. 'People always ask why I wasn't in (1982 movie) *Escape To Victory* with the other Ipswich lads at that time,' he says. 'I remember being on tour with England. That was where I wanted to be.' Mariner later moved to Arsenal in 1984, though he struggled, scoring only 14 goals in 60 League appearances before moving to Portsmouth in 1986. He concluded his playing career at Maltese club, Naxxar Lions.

NOW Assistant coach at MLS side New England Revolution. 'I work with the legendary Steve Nicol,' he says. 'We get on like a house on fire. I got there because I went to Arizona to start my own kids' club. I had about 1,500 kids there by the time I left and I was also working alongside Jürgen Klinsmann at Adidas. After that I was assistant coach at Harvard University in 2002, and then Steve Nicol called up and asked me to join him at New England Revolution. The MLS is taking off. It's a good league and myself and Steve are a good partnership. We're live on the telly these days. But there is one downside to being here: I miss the horse racing at Newmarket.'

Paul Mariner
ENGLAND

39 TONY DALEY

Aston Villa, Wolverhampton Wanderers, Watford, Walsall • 1985-1999

BORN 18 October 1967

POSITION Winger

HONOURS Aston Villa: League Cup Winner 1994

THEN Looking back, Tony Daley is best remembered for a sartorial trademark rather than the fancy ball skills that made him a crowd favourite. As a winger, he burned the touchlines of Aston Villa (1985-1994), Wolves (1994-1998), Watford (1998-1999) and Walsall (1999), even attracting attention at international level – Daley represented England during Graham Taylor's ill-fated Euro '92 campaign in Sweden. But it was his undergarments – a pair of cycling shorts worn beneath the standard issue kit to support the groin and thighs during games – that attracted the most attention. Within weeks of their debut, Sunday League and First Division teams alike were awash with wingers in Lycra leggings. Daley's innovative kit was a necessity, however: it was once reported he could reach speeds of 27 mph while in full flight. Later saw out his career at non-League Forest Green Rovers (1999-2003).

NOW Daley's achievements were always highly regarded – in 1995, Carlton TV released a 30-minute documentary entitled Respect, featuring tributes from John Barnes, former manager Ron Atkinson and team-mate Dwight Yorke. 'I used to play as an out-and-out winger, but now they are few and far between,' says Daley. His involvement in football looks set to continue. Following his retirement, Daley completed a degree in Sports and Exercise Science at Coventry University. He then became a fitness and conditioning coach at Sheffield United. 'Fitness is something I've always been interested in,' he says. 'I completed my Sports Science degree at Coventry University. Whilst I was doing that I was doing the fitness coaching at Forest Green and I was working with the youth academy at Villa.' Left Sheffield United in 2007.

Tony Daley
ASTON VILLA

40 PAUL CANOVILLE

Chelsea, Reading • 1981-1987

BORN 4 March 1962

POSITION Winger

HONOURS Chelsea: Division Two Champions 1984

THEN Chelsea's first ever black player, Canoville was booed by racist fans, not only from rival clubs, but by small sections of the Stamford Bridge crowd. 'It was so full in your face and it was our own fans,' he says. 'I was playing for their club and they were giving me abuse. I was thinking if I just walked outside the gates, what would they do to me? It was frightening. What really hurt so much were the bananas thrown in front of me. I was thinking, ''F**king hell, do you really hate me that much? Do you really not want me to do well for the club?''' In the main, however, Canoville received positive support. He even picked up the nickname 'The King', owing to a peculiar running gait – at times, he resembled a man trying to perch a crown on his head. Sadly, his time at Stamford Bridge coincided with a near relegation to the old Division Three in 1983 and an extended spell in Division Two. Later lost his place to Mickey Thomas before moving to Reading in 1986 where a broken leg banished him to a career in non-League football.

NOW In 1996, Canoville was diagnosed with cancer of the lymph node. 'I was undergoing treatment for a full year,' he says. 'I had a skin condition that needed treatment and when that stopped I had to have chemotherapy and radiotherapy. I knew David Rocastle and when he died of the same illness, that's when I really took note of how serious this had all been.' He overcame the condition but suffered a relapse in 2004. Canoville lost three stone following a larger dose of chemotherapy, but recovered to play for the Chelsea Old Boys against Arsenal in 2006. Has also been assisting Chelsea in their 'Kick Racism out of Football' campaign.

Paul Canoville
CHELSEA

41 GARY MABBUTT

Bristol Rovers, Tottenham Hotspur • 1979-1998

BORN 23 August 1961

POSITION Defender/midfielder

HONOURS Tottenham Hotspur: UEFA Cup Winner 1984, FA Cup Winner 1991

THEN Footballing diplomat who overcame diabetes to win trophies with Spurs while gaining 16 full international caps. Having made his debut for Tottenham at Wembley in the 1982 Charity Shield against Liverpool, Mabbutt went on to become a club legend and served under a string of managers, including Keith Burkinshaw, David Pleat, Terry Venables and Ossie Ardiles. His career was defined by highs and lows: in 1987 he scored the decisive own goal in a 3-2 FA Cup Final defeat against Coventry City (City's main fanzine was subsequently entitled *Gary Mabbutt's Knee*). By 1991, however, he had captained Terry Venables' Spurs team to a 2-1 victory over Nottingham Forest. More spectacularly, he appeared as a drummer on Comic Relief as part of the 'Scouts In Skirts' sketch in 1991. The mind boggles.

NOW Runs his own sports consultancy service called Soccer Services Limited. 'I help football managers to find players and clubs to find managers,' he says. 'But I'm not an agent. A chairman will say to me that he needs a new manager and I'll present him with a dossier of available people who might be suitable, plus the name of their agent so they can be contacted. I've also had nine offers of management, but I've turned them all down.' Also appears on the FA Disciplinary Committee, handing out fines to the likes of Arsene Wenger. 'It's interesting because it throws up all the issues within the game. But if Arsenal are brought before the committee, they will bring their lawyers and they're given the option to have Gary Mabbutt, the ex-Tottenham captain, removed from those proceedings.'

Gary Mabbutt
TOTTENHAM HOTSPUR

42 BRUCE GROBBELAAR

Vancouver Whitecaps (Canada), Crewe Alexandra (loan), Liverpool, Stoke City (loan), Southampton, Plymouth Argyle, Oxford United, Sheffield Wednesday, Oldham Athletic, Chesham United, Bury, Lincoln City • 1979-1998

BORN 6 October 1957

POSITION Goalkeeper

HONOURS Liverpool: FA Cup Winner 1986, 1989, 1992; Division One Champions 1983, 1984, 1986, 1988, 1990; European Cup Winner 1984; League Cup Winner 1982, 1983, 1984

THEN Living evidence that goalkeepers really are different, Grobbelaar was the crazy-legged Liverpool number one who entertained fans and terrified players with his goalmouth antics. These included handstands, penalty area athletics and a wobbly-knee'd routine during the 1984 European Cup Final penalty shoot-out that threw opponents Roma off guard. Before Anfield Grobbelaar had previously worked as a soldier in Rhodesia and even earned a baseball scholarship to America but turned it down to play football. The latter stages of his career were just as colourful: he was left in financial collapse when *The Sun* claimed he had been involved in an alleged match-fixing scam alongside former Wimbledon players, John Fashanu and Hans Segers. The three in 1994 were acquitted, and Grobbelaar pursued a libel case against *The Sun*. This seemed a shrewd move at first – he was awarded £85,000 in damages only for the Court of Appeal to rule this as a miscarriage of justice. This was later overturned and Grobbelaar was awarded £1 in damages and ordered to pay *The Sun*'s £500,000 legal costs. He was officially bankrupt.

NOW Coaches in South Africa, where he has worked with a string of clubs including Hellenic, Manning Rangers and SuperSport United. Also represents the Former Liverpool Players' Association, raising funds for older players by competing in exhibition matches and golf tournaments. 'They were fantastic days at Liverpool,' he says. 'Whatever happens now in my life, I can't complain too much. I came to this country with £10 in my pocket, and after the law lords had finished with me, I had £1. That's quite some life I've had on £9!'

Bruce Grobbelaar
LIVERPOOL

43 CHARLIE COOKE

Aberdeen, Dundee, Chelsea, Crystal Palace, Chelsea, Los Angeles Aztecs (USA), Memphis Rogues (USA), California Surf (USA) • 1960-1981

BORN 14 October 1942

POSITION Winger

HONOURS Chelsea: FA Cup Winner 1970; European Cup Winners' Cup Winner 1971

THEN Charlie Cooke had a habit of being in the right place at the right time during his career. He made his first Chelsea appearance in the Inter-Cities Fairs Cup in 1966 against Barcelona (a 2-0 win), before scoring on his League debut against West Ham. He even had a hand in a Peter Osgood goal during the victorious FA Cup Final replay against Leeds United in 1970. Cooke's career began at Aberdeen (1960-1964) and Dundee (1964-1966), before his move to west London. After six years at the club he moved, briefly, to Crystal Palace (1972-1974), later returning to Stamford Bridge where the once flamboyant Chelsea side of the early 1970s were in decline. Quit England in 1978 for the North American Soccer League (NASL), where he played for the Los Angeles Aztecs, Memphis Rogues and California Surf.

NOW Following his retirement from playing, Cooke remained in America and now runs the Charlie Cooke Soccer School in Cincinnati, Ohio. 'I was at various American clubs after leaving Chelsea in 1978,' he says. 'And I was also the assistant coach to Gordon Jago at Dallas (Tornado) and the coach at Wichita Wings.' Today he recalls the highlight of his career as his appearance in a World XI Select team versus Spain, which was held in the Bernabeu stadium in 1978. And his strangest request from a supporter? 'To sign a programme to put on the graveside of an old Chelsea fan.'

Charlie Cooke
CHELSEA

44 MARK WALTERS

Aston Villa, Glasgow Rangers, Liverpool, Stoke City (loan), Wolverhampton Wanderers (loan),
Southampton, Swindon Town, Bristol Rovers • 1981-2002

BORN 2 June 1964

POSITION Winger

HONOURS Glasgow Rangers: Scottish League Cup Winner 1989, 1991; Scottish Premier League
Champions 1989, 1990, 1991. Liverpool: FA Cup Winner 1992; League Cup Winner 1995

THEN Probing winger who scored 32 goals in 181 League appearances for Aston Villa (1981-
1987). Walters was a Villa fan who quickly cruised through the youth ranks before signing full-time in
1981 and making his first team debut for gaffer Tony Barton in April 1982. His work rate for Villa
drew envious glances from across the border. In 1987, Walters was tempted by Graeme Souness's
offer of a place at Glasgow Rangers as the first black footballer to represent the club. The trophies
began to gather: Walters picked up three Premier League trophies in three seasons (1989-1991)
and earned his only England cap in 1991. A £1.25 million move to Anfield followed, though Walters
failed to replicate the glory days of Ibrox and Villa Park. He was loaned out to
Stoke (1993-1994) and Wolves (1994-1995), before closing his career at
Southampton (1996), Swindon Town (1996-1999) and Bristol Rovers (1999-
2002).

NOW Walters retired from the game in 2002 at the age of 38. Shortly
afterwards he took up a post at Coventry Preparatory School, coaching
children between the ages of four and 11. By 2005 he was a full-time member
of staff, coaching years three to eight. Elsewhere, Walters is the Under-14s
coach at Aston Villa and regularly turns out for the Glasgow Rangers Masters
side. In between playing and coaching commitments, he helps with the 'Kick
Racism out of Football' organisation.

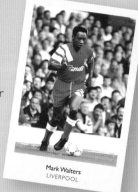

Mark Walters
LIVERPOOL

45 RAY STEWART

Dundee United, West Ham, St Johnstone, Stirling Albion • 1977-1990

BORN 7 September 1959

POSITION Right back

HONOURS West Ham: FA Cup Winner 1980

THEN Despite playing in Scotland and earning 10 international caps, Ray Stewart is best remembered for his time at Upton Park where he was nicknamed 'Tonka' due to his indestructible nature (a term attributed to the pocket-sized vehicles made by Tonka Toys). A fearless right back, Stewart took an impressive 86 penalties during his West Ham career, missing only ten. He even scored 13 goals from the spot in the 1981/82 season. 'I always felt confident of scoring but it wasn't off the cuff,' he says. 'I used to practice religiously and spent hours on the training ground working on my striking of the ball. It got to the stage where, whenever we were awarded a penalty, the fans and my team-mates considered it to be as good as a goal, and I liked being under that pressure.' His goals were occasionally decisive: during the 1981 League Cup Final against Liverpool, Stewart scored the equaliser in a 1-1 draw to take the game to a replay at Villa Park, though Liverpool were to claim the trophy. Overall, he scored 84 goals in 431 West Ham appearances.

NOW Has recently been working as a chauffeur after managing a string of Scottish clubs, including Livingston, Stirling Albion and Forfar Athletic where he was sacked in 2004. Leaving football was hard for Stewart. At the age of 31 he was even advised by West Ham club doctors to retire from the game due to recurring injuries. 'Brian Roper, the club doctor, advised me to call it a day and said that I would never be the same player,' he says. 'I had the chance to take a big insurance pay-off and set myself up, but I couldn't do it. Football was my life and there was no way I could finish like that.'

Ray Stewart
SCOTLAND

46 WAYNE FEREDAY

Queens Park Rangers, Newcastle United, Bournemouth, West Bromwich Albion, Cardiff City
• 1980–1994

BORN 16 June 1963

POSITION Winger

HONOURS None

THEN Quick-from-the-traps winger, who was rumoured to be QPR's fastest ever player. Wayne Fereday made an explosive start to his QPR debut, scoring twice in a 4-0 win over Bristol Rovers in August 1980. 'I remember thinking afterwards how great it was,' he says. 'Being a young lad I thought all the papers would want to talk to me after the game. I got showered and changed and walked outside and everyone had gone, the ground was totally empty. So I walked up to White City and got the tube home.' Later moved to St James' Park in 1989 after making 196 League appearances at the Loftus Road club (scoring 21 goals). Sadly, he failed to make the same impact and was sold onto AFC Bournemouth, later finishing his career at West Brom and Cardiff City. 'Over my time (at Newcastle) I didn't play well in fairness,' he says. 'The Newcastle fans either love you or hate you, there's no in-between and I think I let them get to me. In the end Jim Smith pulled me in and said it wasn't working out and that was that.'

NOW Despite hinting that a career in refereeing was his next vocational choice, Fereday joined up with (news agency) the Press Association, working on Portsmouth games as a match coordinator. Also worked at Cookes furniture store in Christchurch, Dorset. 'The Profressional Footballers' Association asked me if I fancied (refereeing),' he says. 'I think they probably ask everyone when they retire, but at the time I didn't think I had the right personality to do it – I'm too laid back. When I was playing you could talk to the refs and have a bit of a laugh and a joke, but you can't do that these days.'

Wayne Fereday
QUEENS PARK RANGERS

47 TERRY MANCINI

Watford, Port Elizabeth (South Africa), Leyton Orient, Arsenal, Queens Park Rangers, Arsenal, Aldershot • 1961-1977

BORN 4 October 1942

POSITION Centre back

HONOURS Queens Park Rangers: Division Three Champions 1973

THEN Instantly recognisable for his balding pate and Terry Nutkins-style hair which flowed behind him as he operated in the backlines of Arsenal and QPR. A self-confessed player of limited ability, Mancini began business as a centre half at Watford before moving to South Africa and Port Elizabeth. 'The standard of football was probably equivalent to the English Fourth Division,' he says. Mancini later moved to Orient (1967-1971) before signing at QPR for £25,000 in 1971. Once ensconced at Loftus Road, he worked with the likes of Stan Bowles and Terry Venables and helped the club secure promotion to Division One, though a greater surprise was to follow: in 1974 he was transferred to Highbury, once again for £25,000. 'I really felt I had arrived when I stepped out at Highbury and spent the next three seasons with Arsenal, playing with some of the greatest names in the game – Ball, Brady, O'Leary, Stapleton,' he says. He later moved to Aldershot in 1976 before ending his football career in Los Angeles.

NOW Following his retirement, Mancini embarked on a number of business ventures including a sandwich bar, a pub, a betting shop and – bizarrely, given his distinctive image – a ladies' hairdressers. Also worked as assistant manager at Fulham and Luton Town. More recently he has worked in the Corporate and Events Division of Barwell Leisure tour operators, organising tours to La Manga in Spain. Today his football achievements remain a constant surprise. 'I felt I had worked hard enough and achieved more than most would have thought, with the limited ability I had,' he says. 'But the thing that always pushed me further was a belief in my own ability.'

Terry Mancini
QUEENS PARK RANGERS

48 BRENDAN ORMSBY

Aston Villa, Leeds United, Shrewsbury Town (loan), Doncaster Rovers, Scarborough, Wigan Athletic
• 1978-1994

BORN 1 October 1960

POSITION Centre half

HONOURS None

THEN Tough-tackling centre half who made his name first with Aston Villa and then Leeds following a £650,000 transfer in 1986. Ormsby made three appearances in Villa's 1982 European Cup run, though Leeds fans have mixed memories of his time at Elland Road. 'If the Leeds fans can chuck one thing at me,' he says, 'then it's the mistake (a crucial error in possession) I made in the (1986) FA Cup semi-final against Coventry when we were leading 1-0.' Following his spell at Leeds (which was hampered by ligament injuries), Ormsby moved to Shrewsbury on loan (1990), then Doncaster (1990-1992) and Scarborough (1992), before taking over the reins at non-League Waterford in Ireland. 'It was quite amateurish in some ways,' he says. 'The facilities were bad. We were expected to train on car parks and then expected to perform on the pitch. Then in one game I had to take the goalkeeper off just after half-time because he was a big star for Waterford at hurling. That sport is really big over there. Waterford had a hurling semi-final that same day and that took preference. After coming out of our game he was given a police escort in his car to the ground.'

NOW Following his spell at Waterford, Ormsby signed on the dole and began approaching professional football clubs for work. Of the 70 speculative letters posted, he only received 12 replies, though in 1994 Ormsby made two appearances for Wigan Athletic. Later joined the Press Association – reporting on a number of football events including Euro 2000 – and worked for the *Yorkshire Post* for two years in the classified adverts department. Elsewhere, Ormsby has spent several years as a postman because he 'likes being out and about in all sorts of weather' and has worked as a coach at Leeds United.

Brendan Ormsby
ASTON VILLA

49 STEVE WIGLEY

Nottingham Forest, Sheffield United, Birmingham City, Portsmouth, Exeter City • 1981-1993

BORN 15 October 1961

POSITION Winger

HONOURS None

THEN Winger who appeared as a fancy ball player during his time at Brian Clough's Nottingham Forest (1981-1985). Having made his debut at 21, 'Wrigley' (as he was nicknamed by one newspaper reporter) made 82 League appearances and scored two goals, before being transferred to Sheffield United in 1985. Following a disappointing year at the Blades, he joined Birmingham City where one spectacular performance against Portsmouth persuaded Pompey gaffer Alan Ball to bring him to Fratton Park. The following four years drew mixed reviews: Wigley's form was inconsistent and in 1993 he moved to Exeter City.

NOW Until 2007, Wigley was assistant coach at Manchester City until the resignation of former Forest team-mate and City boss, Stuart Pearce. Wigley began his coaching career at Aldershot, before returning to Forest as Assistant Academy Director under David Platt. In 2001, he moved to Southampton, working first as Academy Director while simultaneously working with the England Under-21 framework. Following departures of Saints bosses Gordon Strachan and Paul Sturrock (both in 2004), Wigley stepped in as manager. His second spell in charge lasted a few months. By December 2004 he had been replaced by Harry Redknapp. Later employed by Stuart Pearce at Man City.

Steve Wigley
PORTSMOUTH

50 MARK DENNIS

Birmingham City, Southampton, Queens Park Rangers, Crystal Palace • 1978-1990

BORN 2 May 1961

POSITION Left back

HONOURS None

THEN Marauding full back who earned the 'Psycho' tag (long before Stuart Pearce) thanks to some fairly robust tackling. Dennis was a fearsome opponent during his career, though he's best remembered for a horrific medical condition called decompartmentalisation – a major blood clot in the arteries which nearly ended his life in 1985. Following a 50-50 tackle with Mark Hughes during the 0-0 draw between Southampton and Manchester United, Dennis suffered a dead leg but opted to play on. 'A few beers' followed that night, and his leg doubled in size with swelling. 'The doctors had to split my leg open (to treat the condition),' he says. 'I lost four pints of blood. To make it worse they couldn't stitch my leg up before the swelling went down. I was just laying there for two weeks with an open wound.' The photos of Dennis's gruesome injury later appeared in *The Sun*, though at 23, he made a full recovery. 'I have a hell of a scar,' he says. 'But I always say it's from a shark bite.'

NOW Director of Football at non-League Eastleigh Town. Following retirement, Dennis moved to Spain for two years before battling through personal problems to build a career in coaching. 'I was assistant manager of Fleet for a year,' he says. 'But I've been at Eastleigh for five and a half years now. I love it.' On www.truegreats.com he claims his most memorable moment was 'getting stabbed by my ex-wife.' Elsewhere he remembers his funniest moment in football: 'During warm-up at Old Trafford I told (Saints team-mate) Andy Townsend I was going to hit a young Mark Hughes with a left foot drive. I proceeded to drive it straight into his face and gave him a nose bleed.'

Mark Dennis
CRYSTAL PALACE

51 MEL STERLAND

Sheffield Wednesday, Glasgow Rangers, Leeds United • 1979-1994

BORN 1 October 1961

POSITION Right back/dead ball maestro

HONOURS Leeds United: Division Two Champions 1990; Division One Champions 1992

THEN Solid right back with a powerful free kick, Mel 'Zico' Sterland earned his nickname due to an effective strike rate from set pieces. 'That name came from the fans,' he says. 'I loved it.' He scored 37 goals during his ten years at Wednesday, mainly from dead ball situations before joining the English exodus to Graeme Souness's Glasgow Rangers in 1989. After only nine games (which included three goals), Sterland was on his way back south, this time to Leeds United where he joined former Wednesday manager Howard Wilkinson. This proved a happy marriage: Sterland made 114 League appearances, scoring 16 goals. He also earned his only England cap in 1989 during a friendly against Saudi Arabia. A persistent ankle injury later ended his career in 1994.

NOW Currently retired through illness. 'I went into sales after leaving football,' says Sterland. 'I was selling photocopiers and telephone systems for a company called Concept in Sheffield. Then in 1996 I went on to sell gases like propane for a company called Energas. In 1997 I went into football agency work, but three years ago I was diagnosed with deep vein thrombosis. I struggle to walk up the stairs these days. It's so frustrating.' Also made an appearance in the Sean Bean football flick, *When Saturday Comes* (1996). 'I was supposed to be playing a Sheffield United character. I made sure my Wednesday shirt was underneath the United kit at all times.'

Mel Sterland
GLASGOW RANGERS

52 JIMMY CASE

Liverpool, Brighton & Hove Albion, Southampton, Bournemouth, Halifax Town, Wrexham, Wanneroo British (Australia), Darlington, Sittingbourne (non-League), Brighton & Hove Albion • 1973-1995

BORN 18 May 1954

POSITION Midfielder

HONOURS Liverpool: Division One Champions 1976, 1977, 1979, 1980; UEFA Cup Winner 1976; European Cup Winner 1977, 1978, 1981; League Cup Winner 1981

THEN Artful, 'muzzied' midfielder who stuffed his trophy cabinet with the Liverpool (1973-1981) team of the late 1970s. Case was also reported to have 'the hardest shot in football' following several spectacular long range goals from midfield – the most notable was a cracker in the 1977 FA Cup Final defeat against Manchester United when Case collected the ball, turned and fired home from just outside the area. Following four years at Brighton (1981-1985), which included an FA Cup Final defeat against Man United, Case moved to Southampton (1985-1991) and was made club captain and Player of the Season in 1990. Later saw out his career with brief spells at Bournemouth, Halifax, Wrexham, Darlington and Brighton, plus stints at non-League Sittingbourne and Australian team, Wanneroo British.

NOW After dabbling with management at Brighton and non-League Bashley, Case now splits his time between exhibition matches, the after-dinner circuit and media work with Southampton FC's radio station, The Saint. 'When I play for the Liverpool Masters team, my shooting still packs a punch,' he says. 'I had a pension when I left football, but a lot of players didn't bother, so I'm comfortable financially, but not well off. I still get recognised, but the moustache has gone. Once (former Liverpool player) Mark Lawrenson got rid of his, everyone else did too. My hair's not too bad. Well, put it this way, it's not as bad as my old mate, (ex-Evertonian) Peter Reid.'

Jimmy Case
LIVERPOOL

53 IAN CALLAGHAN

Liverpool, Fort Lauderdale Strikers (USA), Swansea City, Crewe Alexandra • 1960-1982

BORN 10 April 1942

POSITION Midfielder

HONOURS Liverpool: Division One Champions 1964, 1966, 1973, 1976, 1977; European Cup Winner 1977, 1978; FA Cup Winner 1965, 1974; UEFA Cup Winner 1973, 1976; Division Two Champions 1962

THEN Mr Liverpool. Callaghan holds the record for the most Liverpool appearances (640 in the League) during an 18-year career from 1960-1978 and outstayed legendary manager Bill Shankly. Having joined the Reds as a winger in 1960, Callaghan helped Liverpool secure promotion to Division One in 1962, before claiming the in 1964. The 1966 World Cup was a brief distraction: Callaghan was called up to Alf Ramsey's victorious squad, making an appearance in the 2-0 group victory over France at Wembley. At Anfield a trophy glut followed, but Callaghan was virtually made redundant at international level as Ramsey developed the 'Wingless Wonders' formation, though he would play again for England 11 years later at the age of 35. As his career developed, Callaghan moved into central midfield at Anfield, helping Liverpool to their first European Cup in 1977. By 1978, and with one more European Cup secured, Callaghan was on his way to the NASL boom in North America with Fort Lauderdale Strikers (1978), before finishing his career at Swansea (1979-1981) and Crewe Alexandra (1981-1982). Throughout his career he was booked only once.

NOW Works for Littlewoods on the Spot The Ball Panel. Following his departure from football, Callaghan began running pubs in Liverpool with former team-mate, Geoff Strong. 'We took leases off pubs and sold them on,' he says. 'It was quite successful. It also seemed the thing to do when you were an ex-footballer in those days. I'm too old to play the exhibition stuff though – I'll be getting my pension soon. But I do keep in touch with the Former Liverpool Players' Association. I do the secretarial work, so we'll meet up, watch the games and do the meet and greet stuff in the club lounges.'

Ian Callaghan
LIVERPOOL

54 GRAHAM BAKER

Southampton, Manchester City, Southampton, Aldershot (loan), Fulham • 1976-1992

BORN 3 December 1958

POSITION Midfielder

HONOURS None

THEN Robust Saints midfielder. Baker began at Southampton as a junior before making a dream debut in 1977 during a Second Division game against Blackpool – he scored the opening goal in the first minute. A season later, and with the club promoted, Baker was an established first-team regular, playing alongside the likes of Steve Williams in midfield as Saints pressed for Division One stability. Once manager Lawrie McMenemy decided upon the signing of goalkeeper Peter Shilton in 1982, Baker was sold to John Bond's Manchester City for £350,000 to help finance the deal. Following relegation, five years at Maine Road and 117 League appearances between 1982 and 1987, Baker was back at The Dell where he played for three years through niggling injuries before a loan spell at Aldershot and a free transfer to Fulham in 1990. Retired in 1992. 'I was told to stop playing by doctors or I'd end up in a wheelchair,' he says.

NOW Went into coaching at youth level at Carshalton Athletic (1996-1998) and Fulham's youth academy. Another year as assistant coach at Carshalton was followed by a position as Development Officer at Conference side Woking under the management of former Saints team-mate, Glenn Cockerill. Baker temporarily replaced Cockerill following his dismissal in March 2007. Elsewhere, Baker set up the Baker School of Motoring in Cheam in 1992. 'I stopped doing that a couple of years ago,' he says. 'I got my instructor's qualifications at Fulham, but sadly I didn't get to drive any Baby Bentleys.'

Graham Baker
ENGLAND

55 MALCOLM MACDONALD

Fulham, Luton Town, Newcastle United, Arsenal, Djurgardens IF (Sweden) • 1968-1979

BORN 7 January 1950

POSITION Centre forward

HONOURS None

THEN Gap-toothed, free-scoring centre forward. Following spells and goals galore at Fulham (1968-1969) and Luton Town (1969-1971) 'Supermac' was signed up by Newcastle for £180,000 in 1971. His impact was immediate – Macdonald scored a hat-trick on his debut, later topping the club's goalscoring lists for five consecutive seasons. He was impressive at international level too. During one England match against Cyprus he scored all five in a 5-0 victory. Having been sold to Arsenal for £333,333.33 in 1976, he repeated his goalscoring feats as their top scorer for two seasons, before a knee injury ended his career in 1979. In between goal gluts, Macdonald appeared in the televised, celebrity athletics event Superstars, running the 100m in a lightning 10.4 seconds. 'Olympics commentator Ron Pickering was in the crowd,' says Supermac. 'He said to me, "There's only one man in Europe quicker than you. You could represent your country in the Olympics. But then, you're not an amateur."'

NOW Presents a radio show on Century FM with former Boro' legend, Bernie Slaven. 'It's hugely enjoyable,' he says. 'When I was 21 – having just signed for Newcastle – I was told by the Radio 2 golf commentator, Whispering George Bailey that I had a good voice for radio. I did a programme for him on Radio Newcastle – I would record a half-hour show on a Thursday afternoon, but it would go out on Saturday before the kick-off. I started there. I learnt how to project my voice. It also helps that I have a grasp of the English language and I don't say, "You know", or "If you like" every five seconds.'

Malcolm Macdonald
NEWCASTLE

56 RONNIE WHELAN

Liverpool, Southend United • 1979-1996

BORN 25 September 1961

POSITION Midfielder

HONOURS Liverpool: Division One Champions 1982, 1983, 1984, 1986, 1988, 1990; League Cup Winner 1982, 1983, 1984; FA Cup Winner 1986, 1989; European Cup Winner 1984

THEN Effervescent midfielder and scorer of important goals, Ronnie Whelan was an important cog in Liverpool's industrious midfield as they dominated the old First Division in the 1980s. Having taken Ray Kennedy's number five shirt, Whelan scored two in the League Cup Final victory over Spurs in 1982 and another in the League Cup Final a year later. He helped the club to a European, League and League Cup treble in 1984 and the League and FA Cup double in 1986. By 1989, Whelan was team captain, following an injury to defender Alan Hansen. Elsewhere he was impressing at international level, scoring for the Republic of Ireland during the draw against Russia in the 1988 European Championships. By the time of the 1990 Division One championship, however, Whelan's role was reduced mainly through injury. He stayed at Anfield until 1994 before two years at Southend United as player-manager.

NOW Following stints in management at home (Southend) and abroad (Panionios, Greece and Olympiakos Nicosia, Cyprus), Whelan now works on the after dinner circuit. 'Greece was alright,' he says, 'but the game was corrupt. The refs favoured the big teams like Panathinaikos and Olympiakos – you never had a chance. It also happens because a lot of players aren't paid by their clubs – they don't always pay on time – so a player can be bought a little bit. We did OK, though. We got to the quarter finals of the European Cup Winner's Cup against Lazio who were managed by Sven (Goran Eriksson) at the time.'

Ronnie Whelan
LIVERPOOL

57 BRIAN MOORE (1932-2001)

BBC, BBC Radio, The Big Match, On the Ball, Midweek Sports Special • 1963-2001

BORN 28 February 1932

POSITION TV commentator

HONOURS The voice of The Big Match

THEN The warming tones of Brian 'Mooro' Moore accompanied some of football's most spectacular moments during a career that spanned five decades. These included Arsenal's Championship-winning game against Liverpool in 1989 ('It's up for grabs now!') and Ronald Koeman's curling free kick that crashed into the back of the net during Holland's 1994 World Cup inals qualifier against England ('He's going to flick one, he's going to flick one!'). Beginning his career as a BBC correspondent in 1961, Moore became the station's first football correspondent. Later he covered the 1966 World Cup for the BBC and a string of FA Cup Finals and European fixtures featuring English clubs. By 1970, he was transferred to ITV during the World Cup where he later became the voice of football flagship programme, The Big Match. Commentated on England and international games until 1998.

WHAT HAPPENED NEXT? Moore retired from commentating after the 1998 World Cup Final between France and Brazil, though he subsequently appeared on Sky Sports in an interviewing capacity. He died in 2001, coincidentally on the same day that England beat Germany 5-1 in Munich. As a former director of Gillingham FC (Moore was a fan), he has a stand named after him at the club's Priestfield Stadium. A Gillingham fanzine is also named after him in tribute, though the title Brian Moore's Head Looks Uncannily Like London Planetarium is somewhat unflattering (and also a lyric from the Half Man Half Biscuit song, Dickie Davies Eyes).

Brian Moore
THE BIG MATCH

58 BERNIE SLAVEN

Morton, Aidrie, Queen of the South, Albion Rovers, Middlesbrough, Port Vale, Darlington
• 1980-1994

BORN 13 November 1960

POSITION Striker

HONOURS None

THEN Considered by many 'Boro fans to be the club's best ever buy (yes, even better than Abel Xavier), Slaven arrived from Albion Rovers in 1985 for £25,000. The price tag was deceiving. Slaven – top scorer in Scotland that year – had refused to re-sign his Rovers' contract and was working as a part time gardener before 'Boro swooped. After 31 goals in his first season, he was a crowd favourite and picked up the *Daily Record* Golden Boot award. Slaven was soon making waves at international level. He was selected for Jack Charlton's Republic of Ireland squad for the 1990 World Cup in Italy, though in total he only made seven appearances for his country, scoring once. His stats at club level were far more impressive: at Boro' he scored 119 League goals in 297 games, before moving to Darlington (1993) and Port Vale (1994). He retired a year later.

NOW A presenter on Century FM radio. 'I did a bit of coaching when I retired from playing, which I enjoyed,' he says. 'Then a job came up at Century FM in 1996 – one of their regular presenters had used bad language. I've been doing the commentary ever since. It's good for me because I've always been an outspoken character. I like to tell the truth and sometimes the truth hurts. It can be embarrassing, too. I once had to bare my backside in the window of Binns department store in Middlesbrough for a bet. I said on air that 'Boro wouldn't beat United at the Riverside in 1999. If they did I'd flash my backside at Binns. When they did (3-2), I had to go through with it. When I got down there the next week, there were 3,000 people waiting to see my bum. Unbelievable.'

Bernie Slaven
MIDDLESBROUGH

59 MARTIN HAYES

Arsenal, Celtic, Wimbledon (loan), Swansea City • 1985-1994

BORN 21 March 1966

POSITION Winger/striker

HONOURS Arsenal: Division One Champions 1989; League Cup Winner 1987.

THEN A scorer of important goals, Martin Hayes was a left winger-cum striker and originally an understudy to Arsenal's Graham Rix. Having made his debut in 1985 (against Oxford United), his emergence soon coincided with Rix's flagging form – Hayes later made the position his own, scoring 24 goals in the 1986/87 season (12 of them from penalties) while helping George Graham's team to a League Cup Final win over Liverpool the same year. 'We were a hard-working, functional side,' he says. 'We got tagged as being boring, but nobody complained when the trophies came in. And we seemed to get a penalty every other week.' By 1989, however, winger Brian Marwood had joined Arsenal and Hayes became a peripheral figure. In 1990, he joined Celtic for £650,000, though the move was disappointing – Hayes only made seven appearances and was later loaned to Wimbledon (1992) before seeing out his career at Swansea City (1994).

NOW Currently managing Conference South side Bishop's Stortford. 'I've been here since 1999,' he says. 'After retiring professionally, I was messing around playing non-League football with Romford and I began taking training sessions. I got my coaching badges three or four years ago and it's grown since then. I eventually became manager of Bishop's Stortford. The standard of football is quite good in the Conference.' Hayes also briefly worked in the car trade before his commitments with Bishop's Stortford increased. 'When I moved into non-League in 1996 I worked for a Ford garage in north London,' he says. 'I was selling new and used cars before working at Dagenham Motors working with commercial motors. I enjoyed it – it was a nice, nine-to-five job because truck drivers are football fans. There was a lot of good banter.'

Martin Hayes
ARSENAL

60 JAN MOLBY

Kolding IF (Denmark), Ajax (Holland), Liverpool, Barnsley (loan), Norwich City (loan), Swansea City
• 1981-1997

BORN 4 July 1963

POSITION Midfielder/dead ball-specialist

HONOURS Liverpool: Division One Champions 1986, 1990; FA Cup Winner 1986, 1992

THEN A podgy ball-player, Danish international and jailbird with a penchant for scoring net-busting free kicks. Despite his portly physique (throughout his career he lost and gained weight frequently), Jan Molby was a midfield visionary. He also single-handedly orchestrated the 1986 FA Cup Final victory over Everton by creating the first and second goals and pinging the ball from midfield to attack throughout. Signed from Ajax by Joe Fagan for £200,000 in 1984, Molby became a First Division sensation and major player in Liverpool's Double-winning team of 1986, though his ten years at Anfield were interrupted by injury (a broken foot forced him from playing in much of the 1987/88 season) and a three month prison stretch in 1988 for reckless driving. Following loan spells at Norwich and Barnsley (both in 1995), he moved to Swansea, where he later became manager. His link with Liverpool was hard to shift, however: Molby is possibly the only Dane in history to sound like Joey Boswell from Bread, while The Kop still reminisces about a hat-trick of penalties scored against Coventry City in the 1986/87 Littlewoods Cup fourth round replay.

NOW Following several stints in the managerial hotseat (Swansea 1996-1997, Kidderminster Harriers 1999-2002 and 2003-2004, Hull City 2002-2003), Molby established himself as a football co-commentator on Danish station TV2. 'I officially retired from playing in 1997,' he says 'But I'd taken up a post on Danish TV, which I enjoy very much. I'm not the equivalent of Alan Hansen – I don't do much studio work, but I do get to go to all the games and commentate on them live. Ever since 1996 I've been to pretty much every single football championship.' Still plays for the Liverpool Masters side where he retains an unswerving eye for the killer pass.

Jan Molby
LIVERPOOL

61 PAUL ALLEN

West Ham, Tottenham Hotspur, Southampton, Luton Town (loan), Stoke City (loan), Swindon Town, Bristol City, Millwall • 1979-1998

BORN 28 August 1962

POSITION Midfielder

HONOURS West Ham: FA Cup Winner 1980. Tottenham Hotspur: FA Cup Winner 1991

THEN Part of the famous Allen football family tree that included Clive (cousin and Spurs team mate), Martin (cousin, QPR and West Ham), Bradley (cousin, QPR and Charlton) and Les (uncle, Double-winner with Spurs in 1961). Given his background, it probably would have been a disappointment had Paul not made the grade as a First Division footballer. As it was, he broke records in his teens, appearing as the then youngest player to ever appear in an FA Cup Finals when West Ham played Arsenal in 1980. Allen was only 17 years and 256 days old when the Hammers lifted the trophy. His team-mates nicknamed him Baby Face. 'He was barely out of short pants and his voice hadn't broken,' says West Ham skipper, Billy Bonds. By 1985 he'd moved to Spurs for £400,000, linking up with his cousin Clive and playing in two FA Cup finals – one a shock 3-2 defeat against Coventry in 1987, the other a 2-1 win over Nottingham Forest in 1991. This victory marked a career peak. Allen later travelled to Southampton in 1993 and was shifted on loan to Luton Town (1994) and Stoke City (1995) before seeing out his career at Swindon (1995-1997), Bristol City (1997) and Millwall (1997-1998).

NOW Works at the Professional Footballers' Association in the Commercial office. 'I did my coaching badges and worked at the Spurs Academy for a while,' he says. 'I went on one or two events with PFA Commercial office and got involved with them in 2000. One of the projects was the Masters football events. I began working here in a consultancy role which later became a full-time position. After football I took six months out because I had different ideas of what I wanted to do. I had a great career and some weird experiences – playing in the FA Cup Final at 17 was surreal. Playing with my cousin Clive at Spurs was great too. But to beat Arsenal in the 1991 FA Cup semi-final was just a fantastic experience.'

Paul Allen
WEST HAM

62 TERRY FENWICK

Crystal Palace, Queens Park Rangers, Tottenham Hotspur, Leicester City (loan), Swindon Town
• 1976-1995

BORN 17 November 1959

POSITION Defender

HONOURS None

THEN Football bad boy who collected cards at Palace (1976-1980), QPR (1980-1987), Spurs (1987-1993), Leicester City (1990-1991, loan) and Swindon (1993-1995), Fenwick was a much respected defender with a fearsome tenacity. Currently QPR's most capped player, he scored an equalising goal in the West Londoners' defeat in the 1982 FA Cup Final against Spurs, and at 5ft 10in, was also one of the smallest centre backs to play for England. Sadly, these highlights were outweighed by a handful of misdemeanours. Today, Fenwick holds the record for the most bookings in a World Cup finals (three in 1986). He was one of several players to be passed by Diego Maradona in the same competition as he scored the 'Goal of the Century' against England in the quarter-finals. And when he broke the leg of Blackburn Rovers' Paul Warhust while playing for Swindon in the 1993/94 season, one tabloid snapper captured Fenwick smiling after the incident. 'That was all rubbish. I wasn't laughing at that,' he says. 'And I was the first to ring Paul in hospital.' Retired shortly afterwards in 1995.

NOW After taking up managerial posts at Portsmouth (1995-1998), Crystal Palace (assistant manager) and Northampton Town (2003), Fenwick moved to Port Of Spain in Trinidad in 2001 where he managed CL Financial San Juan Jabloteh (2001-2003) in the Trinidad and Tobago Pro League. 'I love it in the Carribean,' he says. 'Bobby Robson recommended me for a job and I got it. The standard of football has improved greatly since I've been here, but it's still not great. There's a huge ex-pat community out here, so I get recognised a lot. People always talk to me about the Maradona goal and I often get the blame for not bringing him down.'

Terry Fenwick
ENGLAND

63 KERRY DIXON

Reading, Chelsea, Southampton, Luton Town, Millwall, Watford, Doncaster Rovers • 1980-1997

BORN 24 July 1961

POSITION Striker

HONOURS Chelsea: Division Two Champions 1984, 1989

THEN Kerry Dixon's mark on the First Division following Chelsea's promotion in 1984 was immediate and impressive: a pile-driving volley against Arsenal at Highbury on the opening day of the season. It marked the start of things to come – Dixon claimed 24 League goals that year, sharing the top scorer's spot with Gary Lineker. To anyone who knew his previous form, this was no great surprise. The striker joined Chelsea from Reading for a whopping £150,000 in 1983. He scored 34 goals in his first season and formed a terrifying partnership with hothead centre forward David Speedie as Chelsea secured the Second Division title. His eye for goal earned England call-ups too (eight games, four goals), but injury later hampered his pace and the international appearances were limited. He was linked with Arsenal, which caused boos at Stamford Bridge ('A low point,' muses Dixon). But after nine years in a schizophrenic Chelsea side (top six finishes, relegation, Second Division champions) he joined Southampton to the tune of £575,000 in 1992 as Chelsea's then second highest scorer behind Bobby Tambling with 193 goals. He was reunited with David Speedie at The Dell for one season, and saw out his career at Luton Town (1993-1995), Millwall (1995-1996), Watford (1996) and Doncaster Rovers (1996-1997).

Kerry Dixon
CHELSEA

NOW Divides his time between managing non-League Dunstable, scouting and Matchday hospitality for Chelsea and working for Chelsea TV. It's a far cry from his playing days when former Chelsea chairman, Ken Bates collected Dixon in his Rolls-Royce shortly before signing him. 'It was a great trip down with Ken,' he says. 'I'd never been in a Rolls-Royce. If you've ever been in one you know what they're like, carpets and fur up the walls, on the doors and everything. All the mod cons. You can do what you want. It was great.'

64 DAVID SPEEDIE

Barnsley, Darlington, Chelsea, Coventry City, Liverpool, Blackburn Rovers, Southampton, Birmingham City (loan), West Bromwich Albion (loan), West Ham (loan), Leicester City • 1978-1994

BORN 20 February 1960

POSITION Striker

HONOURS Chelsea: Division Two Champions 1984

THEN Scour any newspaper cuttings from David Speedie's playing career and you'll find his name affixed with the term 'firebrand'. Certainly, he was a hothead, a player capable of unsettling opponents, managers and team-mates with his quick thinking and short fuse. Meanwhile, on the pitch, his attributes were equally unpredictable: renowned for his work rate, 'Speedo' scored a large number of goals with his head, despite his relatively diminutive height of 5ft 7in. His career high point undoubtedly came at Chelsea (1982-1987) where he developed a profitable understanding with fellow centre forward, Kerry Dixon and winger, Pat Nevin – they scored nearly 200 goals between them in a three-year spell, as Speedie emerged as a Scottish international. A £750,000 move to Coventry City (1987-1991) followed his 47 League goals in 162 Chelsea appearances, though in his latter career he appeared unsettled. Speedie played 12 games at Liverpool (1991), moved to Blackburn (1991-1992), Saints (1992-1993), Birmingham (1992), West Brom (1992), West Ham (1993) and Leicester City (1993-1994).

NOW Works in recruitment and manages non-League Harworth Colliery Institute in the Central Midlands League Premier. 'I got involved in the team really because I drink up here,' he says. 'I only did it because I worked with their Under-11s team, and in pre-season they asked me to take the first team training. I've just taken over from there. I don't think I'm going to do it next season though. I finished playing football in 1994 and I became a football agent for five years. Then in 2000, I began working in recruitment. But I had a great football career – I loved playing for my country. My debut was against England at Hampden, and we won 1-0, which was just brilliant.'

David Speedie
WEST HAM

65 STEVE NICOL

Ayr United, Liverpool, Sheffield Wednesday, Notts County, West Bromwich Albion (loan), Doncaster Rovers • 1979-1999

BORN 11 December 1961

POSITION Defender, though he played in midfield and upfront. Wore the number 4 shirt, regardless of his role.

HONOURS Liverpool: Division One Champions 1984, 1986, 1988, 1990; European Cup Winner 1984; FA Cup Winner 1986, 1989, 1992

THEN In a 1988 interview with *Match* magazine, Steve Nicol revealed that he'd quite like to go to a fancy dress party, 'as a fairy, so I can wave my magic wand.' For the most part he did this quite effectively at Liverpool, sprinkling his sorcery over a watertight defence that lifted trophies for fun in the late 1980s. Nicol also led a charmed life at Anfield following his £300,000 move from Ayr United in 1981. He missed a penalty in the 1984 European Cup Final against Roma, but still collected a winner's medal following the decisive shootout. Twenty seven caps for Scotland included his position in the Mexico '86 squad. And in 1988, he scored a hat-trick against Newcastle despite operating from the back four. He also bore the brunt of dressing room wind-ups – Alan Hansen would often 'interview' him as a spoof newspaper journalist over the phone. 'He used to slay me,' says Nicol.

NOW Head coach at MLS side, New England Revolution. 'I originally started coaching an A-League team called the Boston Bulldogs in 1999 after a friend of mine asked me over. It was a big move for the whole family, but we settled in quite well and then I became player-coach and then later head coach of New England, on a temporary basis at first. I initially followed (former Italian goalkeeper) Walter Zenga, who was coach until 2000. I was made permanent in 2002. It's a good standard of football out here. It's not Premier League standard but it's probably comparable to the Championship. I love managing, but I miss playing – that's the best job in the world. So I guess I've got the second best job in the world right now.'

Steve Nicol
LIVERPOOL

66 MICHAEL THOMAS

Arsenal, Portsmouth (loan), Liverpool, Middlesbrough (loan), Benfica (Portugal), Wimbledon
• 1984-2001

BORN 24 August 1967

POSITION Midfielder

HONOURS Arsenal: Division One Champions 1989, 1991; League Cup Winner 1987. Liverpool: FA Cup Winner 1992; League Cup Winner 1995

THEN 'It's up for grabs now!' When Michael Thomas fizzed an Adidas Tango past Bruce Grobbelaar's despairing clutches during the final game of the 1988/89 season, his place, and ecstatic head-over-heels celebrations, were sealed in football history forever. The goal, which was enough to snatch the title from Liverpool on goal difference, even became the focal point in Nick Hornby's best-selling novel, *Fever Pitch*. Arsenal were equally chuffed – Thomas was earning only £400 a week. 'We were all on peanuts,' he says. Despite subsequent financial advances, his career never matched those heights again. Sure, he won another title with Arsenal in 1991 and picked up two England caps. He moved to Anfield in 1991 and even scored a cracking volley for Liverpool in the 1992 FA Cup Final against Sunderland. But how to match the buzz of a last-second title winner? Certainly not by moving to Graeme Souness's Benfica in 1998, where he was embroiled in a pay dispute, lost his first team spot and became English football's forgotten man. 'It gets lonely out here,' he said in 2000. Thankfully The Crazy Gang were on hand to help and he returned to England for eight games at Wimbledon before retiring in 2001.

NOW Thomas regularly plays for the Liverpool Masters side and runs his own security firm and chauffeur company in Liverpool. 'It's for high-level individuals,' he says. 'We guard presidents and things like that. My wife is from the north, so she likes being in the north, so we're definitely settling in the north. It's a nice way of life, quieter, more peaceful (than London). Evertonians buy me drinks. Liverpudlians buy me drinks. Everybody buys me drinks.'

Michael Thomas
ARSENAL

67 STEVE MCMAHON

Everton, Aston Villa, Liverpool, Manchester City, Swindon Town • 1979-1998

BORN 20 August 1961

POSITION Midfielder

HONOURS Liverpool: Division One Champions 1986, 1988, 1990; FA Cup Winner 1986, 1989

THEN As well as his role in Liverpool's fearsome midfield of the late 1980s, Steve McMahon's career is best remembered for two pivotal moments in defeat. During the title decider of 1989 against Arsenal, McMahon was spotted by cameras, gesticulating at team-mates while informing them that they had 'one minute' to hang on to a one-goal deficit. This result would secure the Championship. Moments later, Arsenal midfielder Michael Thomas popped the ball past Bruce Grobbelaar and the trophy was on its way to Highbury. A year previously, in the 1988 FA Cup Final against Wimbledon, McMahon had been on the end of a vicious Vinnie Jones tackle. The midfield battle was lost and The Crazy Gang caused the biggest upset in Wembley history with a 1-0 win. This is an unfair reflection on McMahon's career, however. Having started as a ball boy-turned-player at Goodison Park (1979-1983) and ensured 'hardman' status at Villa (1983-1985), he solidified Liverpool's midfield between 1985 and 1991. Spells at Manchester City (1991-1994) and Swindon (1994-1998) tailed his career which also included 17 England caps between 1988 and 1991.

NOW McMahon turned to player-management at Swindon (1994-1998) and management at Blackpool (2000-2004). He later moved to Australia to manage Perth Glory FC, though his stint in charge witnessed poor results. He left in 2005. Since then he has signed a contract as a TV pundit with Asian-based TV station ESPN Star Sports. Today he rates an Imre Varadi goal for Everton as one of the funniest moments of his career. 'He ran to what he thought were the Everton supporters,' he says. 'They were, in actual fact, the Liverpool fans. One of them threw a pie straight in his face.'

Steve McMahon
LIVERPOOL

68 MICKEY GYNN

Peterborough United, Coventry City, Stoke City • 1979 – 1993

BORN 19 August 1961

POSITION Midfielder

HONOURS Coventry City: FA Cup Winner 1987

THEN In Panini sticker folklore, Mickey Gynn was the Coventry City midfielder with a Freddie Mercury 'tache and Smurf physique. To anyone who followed his Highfield Road career throughout the 1980s – particularly during the Sky Blues' victorious FA Cup run of 1987 – he was a highly influential ball player who carved out a series of chances, most notably in the 1987 Cup Final at Wembley when City overturned Spurs. 'That was the highlight of my career,' he says. 'The FA Cup run was amazing, but the final was a cracking game and it really put us on the map. It's amazing, even though we played top-flight football for ten years, to win an FA Cup Final was brilliant. I then went to Stoke City for a couple of years but I picked up a bad toe injury and I retired in 1993. I just couldn't play full-time.'

NOW Up until two years ago, Gynn was still playing non-League football for a number of clubs, including Kettering Town. 'I'm a postman now,' he says. 'I work in Ryton-on-Dunsmore and it's just by the Coventry training ground, which is ironic. I got into the post straight after football. When I stopped playing I realised I had to earn some money. After playing football for so long I decided that I needed an outdoor job and being a postman seemed perfect. I use it as a training session really.' Gynn also works for the Professional Footballers' Association, providing match statistics. 'They give us a mobile phone and a headset and I relay info back to a central office. It keeps me in touch with the game.' And the moustache? 'No, I shaved it off,' he says. 'I wish I'd shaved it off in the 1980s. It was horrendous.'

Mickey Gynn
STOKE CITY

69 RAY WALLACE

Southampton, Leeds United, Swansea (loan), Reading (loan), Stoke City, Hull City, Airdrie
• 1988-1999

BORN 2 October 1969

POSITION Full back

HONOURS None

THEN The big time seemed to pass Ray Wallace by. While his brothers scored fame and fortune for Southampton and then Man United (Danny) and Leeds (twin brother, Rodney), Ray was forever in their shadow, despite moving to Leeds (1991-1994) at the same time as his twin. Once at Stoke City (1994-1999) he enjoyed an upturn in fortunes, and fans of the club remember him for his impressive work rate as a full back and defensive midfielder. 'In a way it was hard playing with my brothers at Southampton,' he says. 'Everyone thought we would have similar styles of play, which wasn't the case – we all played in different positions. It was great fun when we were on the same pitch together. Playing in the same team as Rod and Danny was a great feeling. The family were really chuffed. My mum and dad came to our first match against Sheffield Wednesday. It was a historic day.' Finished his career with a handful of appearances at Hull City and Airdrie in 1999.

NOW Ray has been a fitness instructor for several years. 'I retired in 1999 and in 2000 I got my professional fitness qualifications and started work at Fitness First in Wigan. I now work in a gym in Chorley. I'm qualified to give gym instruction and sports therapy, provide rehab and sports massages and different types of training as well as first aid. I worked at Bolton's youth academy in 2003/2004 which was good fun. People do recognise me – but they always think I'm Danny.'

Ray Wallace
AIRDRIE

70 STEVE FOSTER

Portsmouth, Brighton & Hove Albion, Aston Villa, Luton Town, Oxford United, Brighton & Hove Albion • 1975-1996

BORN 24 September 1957

POSITION Defender

HONOURS Luton Town: Littlewoods Cup Winner 1988

THEN Along with tennis superbrat John McEnroe, 'Fozzie' emerged in the 1970s and 1980s as a sportsman synonymous with the sweatband. This was worn below his voluminous curls to menacing effect, though there was more to the imposing centre half than mere sartorial ingenuity. Having played for Portsmouth between 1975 and 1979, Foster moved around the coast to Brighton & Hove Albion (1979-1984) and enjoyed considerable success, playing in the 1983 FA Cup Final replay defeat against Manchester United and earning an England call up to the 1982 World Cup in Spain, where he joined the likes of Bryan Robson, Steve Coppell and Kevin Keegan. Sadly he only claimed three caps under England gaffer Ron Greenwood. A disappointing £200,000 transfer to Aston Villa took place in 1984 (he lasted only eight months and 15 games), but Foster was back to his bruising best at Luton Town as the Kenilworth Road outfit took the First Division's fancy dans to task on their plastic pitch. He lifted the Littlewoods Cup in 1988 as captain following a Wembley showdown against Arsenal before moving to Oxford United (1989-1992). He returned to Brighton in 1992 for the final four years of his career.

NOW Stripped of his headband, Foster now runs his own insurance firm. 'I set a company up called Pro Secure when I retired,' he says. 'Our speciality is looking after footballers and we insure 4,000 professional players through the Professional Footballers' Association. Obviously, we look after them in event of injury and accident. We also look after a lot of footballers in Spain, too.'

Steve Foster
BRIGHTON & HOVE ALBION

71 PAUL DAVIS

Arsenal, Stabaek (Norway), Brentford • 1979-1995

BORN 9 December 1961

POSITION Midfielder

HONOURS Arsenal: League Cup Winner 1987, 1993; Division One Champions 1989, 1991; FA Cup Winner 1993; European Cup Winners' Cup Winner 1994

THEN Then a composed Arsenal midfielder, Davis promised a huge England future without making it past the Under-21s. He was a Highbury talisman, though this had as much to do with his debut appearance (a 2-1 win over Spurs at White Hart Lane in 1980) as it did with his role in securing two First Division titles. Certainly, Davis was predominately a one-club man, serving at Arsenal from 1980 to September 1995, where he made 351 League appearances and scored 30 goals. When he was ultimately released, he moved first to Norwegian club Stabaek (to regain his match fitness) and then to Brentford, though he played for less than a season before retiring through injury. Notoriously, he is probably best remembered for the jaw-breaking punch he delivered to Saints midfielder Glenn Cockerill during Arsenal's clash with Southampton at Highbury in 1988. The Balboa style uppercut – which was missed by both the referee and his assistants – was the first football incident to be trialled by TV. Davis was slapped with a then record nine-game ban and £3,000 fine. Ouch.

NOW Following his retirement from the game in 1995, Davis became a youth coach at Arsenal until 2003. By 2005 he was appointed as coach at non-League Kettering Town alongside controversial ex-England star Paul Gascoigne. Gazza lasted only six weeks in the position and Davis departed with him in December 2005. He has also held the post of Football Development Officer at the Professional Footballers' Association. Here he has been active in 'encouraging more ethnic minority coaches and players in the professional ranks to take their qualifications'.

Paul Davis
ARSENAL

72 STEVE PERRYMAN

Tottenham Hotspur, Oxford United, Brentford • 1969-1990

BORN 21 December 1951

POSITION Defender/midfield 'destroyer'

HONOURS Tottenham Hotspur: FA Cup Winner 1981, 1982; UEFA Cup Winner 1972, 1984; League Cup Winner 1971, 1973

THEN Spurs' 'Captain Fantastic', Perryman made a record 866 appearances in all competitions. He emerged under legendary manager Bill Nicholson's tutelage in the late 1960s, before making a huge impression on the team during the cup runs of the early 1970s and 1980s, mainly because of his tireless running and play-breaking tackles. 'He had endless stamina,' said Nicholson. 'He was the engine room of the midfield. He will run from the start of a game until the end.' Despite captaining the club for ten years in a notable 17 year career, Perryman made only one England appearance – against Iceland in June 1982. The goals were few (only 39), but when they came they were important: he scored both goals in Spurs' 2-1 win over A.C. Milan in the 1972 UEFA Cup semi-final. His years of service were rewarded with a free transfer in 1986 to Oxford United and then Brentford before becoming player-manager at Griffin Park.

NOW Following managerial spells at Watford, Spurs (as assistant manager to Ossie Ardiles) and I.K. Start in Norway (1994-1995), Perryman moved to Japan where he managed J. League sides Shimizu S-Pulse (1996-2000) and Kashiwa Reysol (2001-2002). Prior to his spell abroad he picked up an MBE for his services to football in 1986. He is currently the Director of Football at Exeter City where he has worked since 2003. Japan proved to be one of his most rewarding experiences, however. 'You had players that really responded to your messages and wanted to improve,' says Perryman in 2005. 'From a satisfaction aspect, it was wonderful. These players didn't want to leave the training ground.'

Steve Perryman
TOTTENHAM HOTSPUR

73 PETER MARINELLO

Hibernian, Arsenal, Portsmouth, Motherwell, Fulham, Phoenix Inferno (USA), Hearts, Partick Thistle
• 1968-1984

BORN 20 February 1950

POSITION Forward/right winger

HONOURS None

THEN Dubbed 'The New George Best' by the British tabloids while at Hibernian, Peter Marinello possessed all the hedonistic attributes of the Manchester United genius, and flashes of the talent. Sadly, the former was to overshadow the latter. Having signed for Arsenal in 1970 for £100,000 (a then club record), Marinello scored on his debut. But things took a turn for the worse and his taste for the high life soon affected his play: he only made three appearances in Arsenal's Double-winning side of 1971 and eventually left for Portsmouth in 1973, notching up a mere 38 League games. 'I made the mistake of chasing the money and would never be the same player again,' he says. Marinello then strung out his career at Motherwell (1975-1978), Fulham (1978-1980), Phoenix Inferno (1980-1981), Hearts (1981-1983) and finally Partick Thistle (1983-1984). 'I finished my career in Scotland, knowing I'd never fulfilled my potential,' he says.

NOW Recently published his autobiography, *Fallen Idle*, Marinello now lives in Bournemouth where he works in youth football. In 1994 he was declared bankrupt when poor business decisions cost him dear. Worse, his son became a drug addict and his wife fell ill. 'I lost £300,000 on a nightclub venture,' he says. 'I buried myself in drink and gambling … I was handed a bankruptcy order in 1994. When I told the court about my dealings it sounded like a joke. I've been through some troubling times, but I can't wait to have some grandchildren to tell them all my stories.'

Peter Marinello
ARSENAL

74 TERRY BUTCHER

Ipswich Town, Glasgow Rangers, Coventry City, Sunderland • 1976-1993

BORN 28 December 1958

POSITION Defender

HONOURS Ipswich: UEFA Cup Winner 1981. Rangers: Scottish Premier League Champions 1987, 1989, 1990; Scottish League Cup Winner 1988, 1989

THEN An iconic England defender best remembered for his blood-splattered performance against Sweden in a World Cup qualifier in 1989. Having suffered a serious head wound in the early stages of the game, Butcher opted to play on. Blood later soaked the bandage affixed to his wound, drenching his shirt and splattering the ball with every header. Away from the blood and gore, Butcher was an uncompromising defender, first coming to prominence with Bobby Robson's successful Ipswich Town team (1976-1986). Following the 1986 World Cup and his role in England's back four, Butcher joined the English player drain to Glasgow Rangers (1986-1990) where he shouldered the likes of Mark Hateley to secure domestic glory. At 31 he became player-manager of Coventry City (1990-1992) and appeared six times before retiring from playing. He re-registered himself two years later when he became player-coach of Sunderland (1992-1993).

NOW Having managed at Coventry and Sunderland, Butcher took the hot seat at Motherwell (2002-2006) after being assistant to manager Eric Black throughout 2001. Despite battling against financial difficulties, he steered the team to a Scottish League Cup Final in 2005 where they were defeated by Rangers 5-1. Later he moved to Australia to coach Sydney FC. He returned to England with Brentford in 2007. And the bloody shirt from that Sweden game? 'I kept both shirts I wore that day,' he says. 'One's up at the Scottish Football Museum in Glasgow, and the other one I think is at home. It's not bloody anymore, though – my wife washed it actually washed up quite well.'

Terry Butcher
GLASGOW RANGERS

75 SAINT ...

Motherwell, Liverpool, Coventry City, Tranmere Rovers • 1958-1973

BORN 7 June 1938

POSITION Forward/midfielder

HONOURS Liverpool: Division One Champions 1964, 1966; FA Cup Winner 1965; Division Two Champions 1962. ITV: World Of Sport, Saint and Greavsie, Sport In Question

THEN As a player, The Saint was a Liverpool legend. He scored all three goals in a 4-3 defeat against Everton in the Senior Cup Final on his debut and went on to grab 95 goals in 336 League matches. He had a knack of scoring in important games too – he scored the winner against Leeds United in the 1965 FA Cup Final. And when Liverpool won the League title in 1964, he weighed in with 19 goals. Following an impressive spell at Anfield he moved to Coventry City in 1971 for one season, before playing a final campaign at Tranmere Rovers and retiring from the game in 1973. Since then he has tried his hand at football management (Motherwell, Portsmouth, Sheffield Wednesday), though his most significant role came as the laughing sidekick to Jimmy Greaves on the ITV magazine show, Saint and Greavsie.

NOW Retired. The Saint started a series of soccer schools after his playing career, but these are now looked after by his son. 'I started the camps when Bobby Moore asked me to do one, way, way back in the 1980s,' he says. 'I ran a couple for him. I was doing that before I worked with Jimmy Greaves. Saint and Greavsie finished in 1992 and then I did Sport In Question, which was a great programme. I don't know why they pulled the plug on that. I still keep in touch with Greavsie. He's fine. We do similar things – a bit of after-dinner speaking, play a bit of golf. Saint and Greavsie was a great show – people enjoyed watching it, we enjoyed doing it and it was a change from the norm. It was a real laugh, but we were serious when we needed to be. In the main it was funny because Jimmy was a very funny guy. It could have run for longer, but Sky had bought the football TV rights and ITV didn't have any League football, so it stopped.'

Ian St. John
LIVERPOOL

76 ... AND 'GREAVSIE'

Chelsea, A.C. Milan, Tottenham Hotspur, West Ham • 1957-1971

BORN 20 February 1940

POSITION Striker

HONOURS Tottenham Hotspur: FA Cup Winner 1962, 1967; European Cup Winners' Cup Winner 1963. ITV: Saint and Greavsie, Sporting Triangles

THEN To one generation of football fans, Jimmy Greaves was a goal-scoring phenomenon, bagging 357 goals in English football for Chelsea, Spurs and West Ham including 25 hat-tricks and 35 FA Cup goals, not to mention 44 England goals in 57 appearances. He also began England's 1966 World Cup campaign as one of Sir Alf Ramsey's preferred strikers before injury ended his tournament. To a younger generation, however, Greaves was one half of the TV duo, Saint and Greavsie – a TV partnership with former Liverpool star, Ian St. John who presented LWT's irreverent Saturday lunchtime football magazine in John Craven knitwear. Running for ten years, the programme featured serious interviews, match analysis and Greavsie's 'hilarious' jibes at Scottish goalkeepers. When Sky TV nabbed the rights to Premiership football, Saint and Greavsie's future was in jeopardy – the partnership was deemed not 'serious enough'. Matters weren't helped with some light-hearted jokes at the expense of Sky during ITV's Euro '92 coverage. Saint: 'Have you got Sky, Jim?' Greavsie: 'No, but the neighbours think I have because I've nailed the wok to the gable end.' Perhaps it was for the best.

NOW Currently works on the after theatre circuit, regaling audiences with his football exploits. The cult of Saint and Greavsie has yet to be revived, however. 'We had a lovely relationship,' says Greavsie. 'But it was a working one. Ian lives in the Wirral and I'm in Essex so, other than work, we didn't see much of each other, but we got on very well. We went abroad for the programme and I loved it. Ian has got a great sense of humour and so we did laugh a lot. Saint and Greavsie became a legendary television show. It was a cult and I don't think there has been anything like it before or since. We used to kick it about and really work and no, I never paid Saint to laugh!'

Jimmy 'Greavsie' Greaves
SAINT AND GREAVSIE

77 CLYDE BEST

West Ham, Tampa Bay Rowdies (USA), Portland Timbers (USA), Feyenoord (Holland), Portland Timbers (USA), Toronto Blizzard (Canada) • 1969-1982

BORN 24 February 1951

POSITION Striker

HONOURS None

THEN Originally from Bermuda (he earned his first cap at the age of 15), Best was one of the first black players to compete in English football after the Second World War. As a muscular centre forward, he possessed physical and mental strength by the bucket load, though Best was often on the end of racial abuse during his time at Upton Park between 1969 and 1976. 'People ask me about the race thing a lot,' he says. 'But I have always said that the ball does not care what colour you are.' Following seven years in London's East End, he joined the player drain to America's newly formed NASL in 1975. 'I was lucky enough to play regularly against some of the best players in the world during that time. Players like Pelé, George Best, Johan Cruyff, and Franz Beckenbauer. As a footballer you can't beat that.'

NOW In 2006, Best was awarded an MBE in the January New Year's Honours List because of his work in football. Prior to that he established his own cleaning service ('Where there's muck, there's money,' he says) before coaching the Bermuda national team in 1997. He left the position in 1999 and took up a job in the Bermuda Prison Service. 'My late father always taught me you have to give something back,' he told *FourFourTwo*. 'I still watch a lot of football in Bermuda as we get Sky Sports, ESPN and Fox Sports. Of course, I'll always be a West Ham fan. Once you've played in the claret and blue you can never get away from it.'

Clyde Best
WEST HAM

78 COLIN GIBSON

Aston Villa, Manchester United, Port Vale, Leicester City, Blackpool, Walsall • 1978-1995

BORN 6 April 1960

POSITION Left back/midfield

HONOURS Aston Villa: Division One Champions 1981; European Cup Winner 1982

THEN Attacking full back who could slot into midfield when required, Gibson began his career at Aston Villa (1978-1985). During seven years he made 185 League appearances, scoring 10 goals despite competing, at times, for his left back spot with the impressive Gary Williams. The work came with rewards: in two years Gibson had helped Villa to a League title and a European Cup, though he didn't make it onto the pitch for the final. His pacy runs up and down the touchline soon drew the attentions of Alex Ferguson who took Gibson to Manchester United in 1985 for £275,000. Though he was at the club for five years, he was a peripheral figure after three campaigns – following a cruciate ligament injury, Gibson only made eight League appearances after the 1987/88 season. Later made over 60 appearances for Leicester City (1990-1994) and ended his career with Walsall (1994-1995) and Blackpool (1995).

NOW Currently a football agent, though Gibson is looking to change career paths. 'I've been an agent for a while now,' he says. 'My last agency, Football First was bought out – we looked after Alan Smith and Gareth Barry. I worked with the Professional Footballers' Association for seven years, and I've also been doing a bit of this and that – property, entrepreneurial work I suppose. It's not quite (property show) Homes Under The Hammer, but it's interesting. At the moment I haven't got a plan for where I want to go next, but I'm thinking about moving to Spain. I still play for the Aston Villa All Stars, but I don't get recognised anymore, I haven't got any hair!'

Colin Gibson
MANCHESTER UNITED

79 COLIN PATES

Chelsea, Charlton Athletic, Arsenal, Brighton & Hove Albion • 1979-1995

BORN 10 August 1961

POSITION Defender

HONOURS Chelsea: Division Two Champions 1984

THEN As a sturdy defender, Colin Pates had an impressive start to his Chelsea career, featuring in a 7-3 victory over Leyton Orient in 1979. It was a taste of things to come – Chelsea embarked on a topsy- turvy adventure through the Leagues, with Pates steering the team as captain, most significantly during the Division Two Championship-winning season of 1984. He was sold to Charlton in 1988 for £400,000 following 281 League appearances for the Stamford Bridge club, before moving to Highbury for £500,000 in 1990. It was clear that Pates' best days were behind him, however, and after struggling to make the first team at Arsenal he was loaned out to Brighton, before making a permanent move in 1993. Retired from the game two years later.

NOW Head of football at Whitgift School in Croydon since 1996. 'I'm in charge of 1,100 boys,' he says. 'I coach cricket and football and pretty much everything else in the sports department. I left Brighton, got my millions of qualifications and went straight into it. It's a top school and I really enjoy being here. The kids know who I am as well. I think it makes a big difference when you have someone coaching you who has actually played the game. And there's a lot more Chelsea fans these days. I still meet up with the Chelsea vets. We get drunk on a regular basis and go down memory lane on the pitch. I've still got it (on the ball) – you never lose it. I didn't have the yards to lose in the first place, but when you're on the pitch you know where you should be, but your legs can't take you there. Plus half of the former players are old and have bad injuries now.'

Colin Pates
ARSENAL

80 DAVID MAY

Blackburn Rovers, Manchester United, Huddersfield Town (loan), Burnley • 1988-2004

BORN 24 June 1970

POSITION Centre back/right back

HONOURS Manchester United: Premier League Champions 1996, 1997, 1999; FA Cup Winner 1996, 1999; Champions League Winner 1999

THEN Ask any Manchester United fan of their enduring memory of the 1999 Champions League Final against Bayern Munich and chances are you'll be regaled with the recollections of Ole and Teddy's last-gasp goals. But somewhere among the reminiscing, somebody is bound to mention the gurning celebrations of United fringe player, David May. Despite hardly featuring in the club's European campaign (and very much a bit part player for large chunks of his Old Trafford career), May led the celebrations as if he'd won the trophy single-handedly. 'I was a bit of a joker in the United dressing room,' he says. 'Some saw that as my biggest joke.' May started his career at Blackburn Rovers in 1988 and was sold to United for £1.4 million in 1994. Despite an impressive trophy haul, May was a bench player for the most part (he made only 123 League appearances between 1994-2003), and was eventually sold to Burnley in 2003 where he retired after a season.

NOW Currently a wine importer. 'I was lucky to have made some money from football to invest in a business,' he says. 'Whereas I played with lads in Burnley who now work in factories. New clients can be surprised I work in the wine industry,' he told *FourFourTwo*, 'but I haven't met an irate Leeds or Liverpool fan who doesn't want to do business. We've also launched a new range, Mayson Ridge – the May coming from my name.' He can also be found working on MUTV or in the Manchester United hospitality suites on matchdays. 'I still jump for every header,' he says.

David May
MANCHESTER UNITED

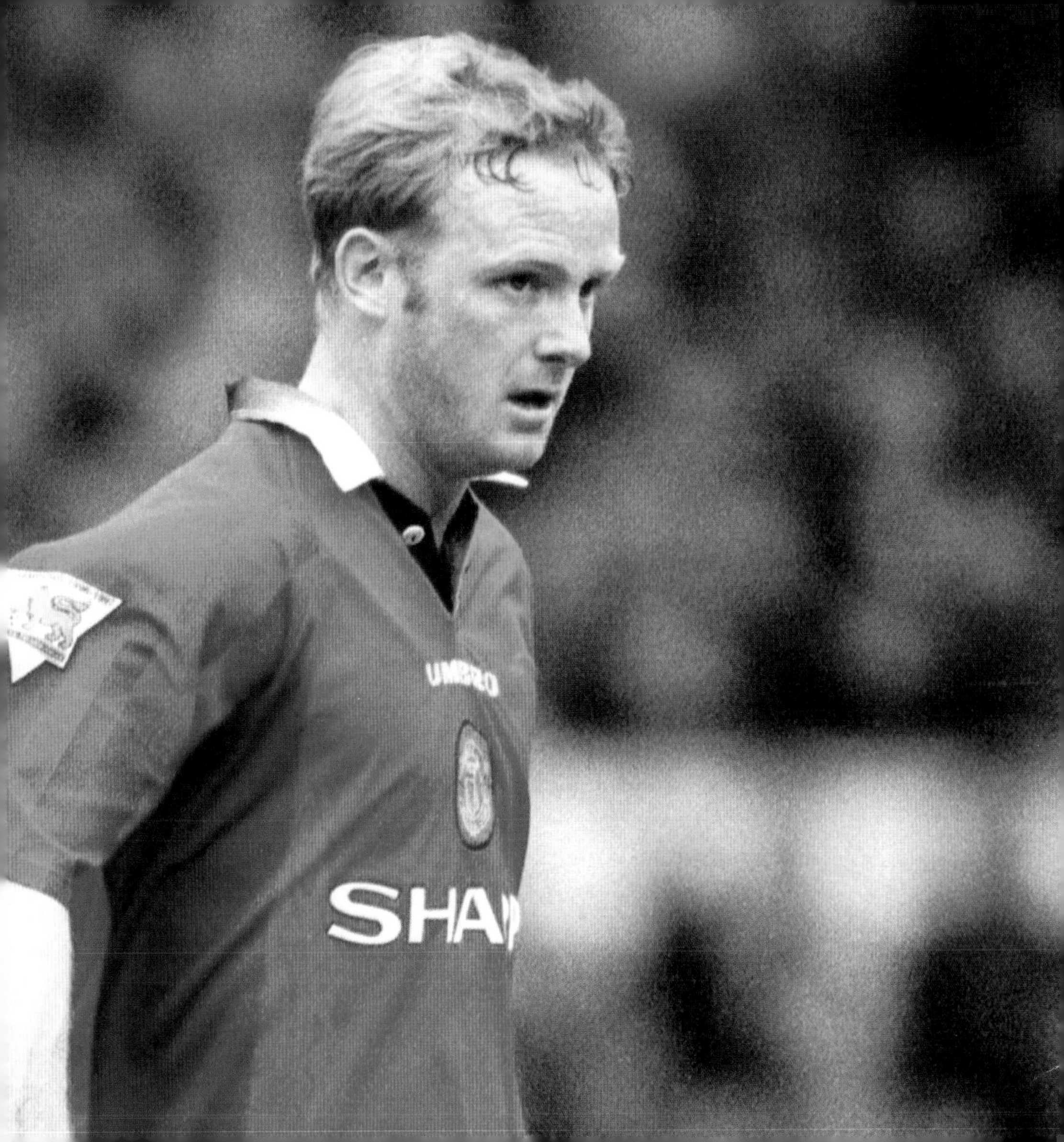
UMBRO
SHA

81 DES BREMNER

Hibernian, Aston Villa, Birmingham City, Fulham, Walsall • 1972-1990

BORN 7 September 1952

POSITION Midfielder

HONOURS Aston Villa: Division One Champions 1981; European Cup Winner 1982

THEN Des Bremner joined Aston Villa at the right time. Having played for Hibs (1972-1979) for seven years and earning only one Scottish cap (when he came on for Kenny Dalglish in the game against Switzerland in 1976) he moved to the Midlands for £275,000 in 1979. One season later, Bremner was an ever present in the side as Villa became Division One champions in 1981. By 1982 he was a European winner. In 1984 he jumped ship, joining former Villa manager Ron Saunders at fierce rivals Birmingham City. His impact was apparent there, too – Bremner assisted in steering Birmingham back to the old Second Division before moving to Fulham in 1989. Played for one more year before moving to Walsall (without a contract) and retiring in 1991.

NOW Currently works in the financial division of the Professional Footballers' Association. 'I'm a financial adviser. I got the opportunity to work with the PFA's financial management in 1991 and it started from there. I advise players on all sorts of things from investments to pensions. I tell players how to plan for the future. I was never a Carol Vorderman with the numbers, but I'm not too bad. As far as my career highlights are concerned, they would have to be winning the League with Aston Villa and the European Cup the following year. They were two great occasions, and to be involved with the great Aston Villa team of that era was a real honour. We caught up recently – it's hard to believe that it was 25 years ago.'

Des Bremner
ASTON VILLA

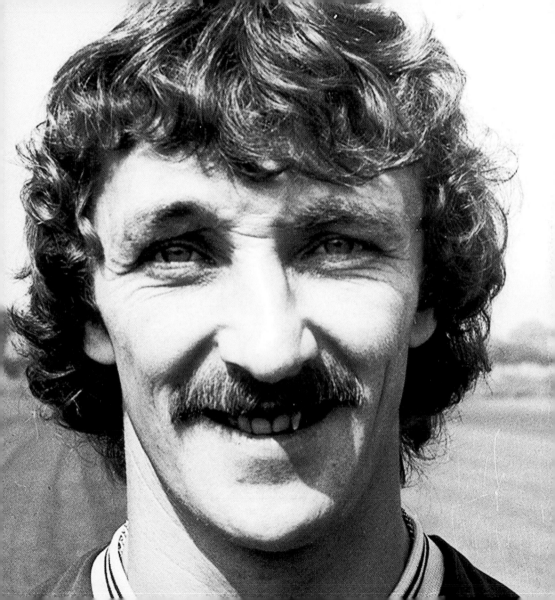

82 GRAEME SHARP

Dumbarton, Everton, Oldham Athletic • 1977-1997

BORN 16 October 1960

POSITION Striker

HONOURS Everton: FA Cup Winner 1984; Division One Champions 1985, 1987; European Cup Winners' Cup Winner 1985

THEN Powerful striker with an adhesive first touch and aerial muscle, Graeme Sharp enjoyed 11 healthy years at Everton where he became a leading club scorer, second only to the legendary Dixie Dean. In a spell that ran from 1980-1991, he partnered a number of prolific hitmen, including Andy Gray and Gary Lineker, and collected Division One, FA Cup and European winners' medals. Bestowed with cult status at Dumbarton – despite his brief appearances at a young age – Sharp moved to Merseyside for £120,000 in 1980. Over a decade later he was sold to Oldham in 1991, where he was made player-manager in 1994 before quitting the game in 1997. Also earned 12 Scotland caps and made one appearance in the 1986 World Cup Finals.

NOW After managing Bangor City in 1998, Sharp embarked on a career with Liverpool's local media. He is also Fans' Liaison Officer at Goodison Park. 'I'm working on the charity and PR side of things as well,' he says. 'As a Liaison Officer I deal with the fans' queries and problems with things like tickets. Plus the club is also involved in a lot of charity work which I help with. The opportunity came up a while ago and I was very interested. I'd played at the club for quite a while and Everton has always been close to my heart. To still be involved is fantastic. I also do a radio show, five nights a week on Century FM alongside Mickey Thomas, formerly of Man United, and Alan Kennedy of Liverpool. So that keeps me busy and it's a good crack.'

Graeme Sharp
OLDHAM ATHLETIC

83 KEVIN BEATTIE

Ipswich Town, Colchester United, Middlesbrough • 1971-1982

BORN 18 December 1953

POSITION Defender

HONOURS Ipswich Town: FA Cup Winner 1978

THEN Kevin Beattie's career is often regarded as an underachievement. As a youngster in Bobby Robson's title-chasing Ipswich team, he collected admirers on a seemingly weekly basis: 'The new Bobby Moore', 'The Diamond' and 'Better than Duncan Edwards' were just some of the accolades bestowed upon him, though his medal cabinet remained empty in comparison – he earned a 1978 FA Cup winners' medal, but missed the 1981 UEFA Cup Final through injury. It was an auspicious start, however. After working his way into Robson's plans, Beattie became the inaugural PFA Young Player of the Year in 1974 and made his England debut in 1975 (later scoring what is considered one of the 50 best England goals of all time when England beat Scotland 5-1), but injury curtailed his career. Niggling knee and back problems, twinned with unfortunate accidents (he once hurt himself in a bonfire), reduced his Ipswich appearances and Beattie only totalled nine England caps, which was a waste given that many expected him to be England's most capped player. Retired through injury in 1982 and attempted two underwhelming comebacks with 'Boro and Colchester the same year, but the end had arrived.

NOW At first Beattie struggled to accept that his career was finished. Despite drinking problems, one suicide attempt and a collapsed pancreas, he's since overcome his career disappointments and has worked as both a scout and a coach; he can also often be found performing on the after-dinner circuit. For the most part he lives off disability benefits. 'I was born too early,' he says. 'I look at the lads now and have to say that £100,000 is a lot to earn in a year, let alone a week.' One little known story: Beattie once defeated Sylvester Stallone in an arm wrestling competition during the making of football flick, *Escape To Victory*. 'He was an arrogant sod,' says Beattie.

Kevin Beattie
IPSWICH TOWN

84 KEVIN SHEEDY

Hereford United, Liverpool, Everton, Newcastle United, Blackpool • 1976-1994

BORN 21 October 1959

POSITION Winger

HONOURS Everton: Division One Champions 1985, 1987; European Cup Winners' Cup Winner 1985

THEN Usually found on the Everton wing, Sheedy was renowned for arcing laser-sighted passes into the opposition's penalty area as part of Howard Kendall's effective team of the 1980s. During a ten-year spell, he collected two First Division titles (1985, 1987), and a European Cup Winners' Cup (1985), though he missed the 1984 FA Cup Final through injury. But it was his ability from a dead ball situation that really placed Sheedy on the football map. Having started at Hereford in 1976, he quickly made his name as a creative winger, before Liverpool bought him in 1978. Once at Anfield, he only made three League appearances in four years before moving to neighbours Everton for £100,000. Given that Sheedy was a fringe player, this transfer didn't raise too many murmurs, though Liverpool fans were to rue his departure – in 274 appearances for the Toffees, Sheedy scored 67 goals. Further success was to come at international level. Sheedy played for the Republic of Ireland and later went on to win 45 caps for his country. By 1992, however, he was surplus to requirements at Goodison Park and moved on a free transfer to Newcastle (1992-1993). Ended his career at Blackpool (1993-1994).

Kevin Sheedy
EVERTON

NOW Since retiring from football, Sheedy has taken assistant manager roles at Tranmere Rovers and Hartlepool United. He is currently on the Everton coaching staff. 'I'm the youth coach here,' he says. 'I work with the 16 to 18 year-olds. I finished playing and went into coaching at Tranmere – with John Aldridge – and Hartlepool. Then I was asked if I'd like to be youth coach at Everton. Obviously, with my history at the club, it was a job I couldn't refuse. I still get a lot of attention from the fans. I go to a lot of games and I'm always being asked about certain incidents - matches, free kicks, goals.'

85 BRIAN TALBOT

Ipswich Town, Toronto Metros (Canada, loan), Arsenal, Watford, Stoke City, West Bromwich Albion, Fulham, Aldershot • 1970-1992

BORN 21 July 1953

POSITION Midfielder

HONOURS Ipswich: FA Cup Winner 1978. Arsenal: FA Cup Winner 1979

THEN Despite playing for a string of clubs and gaining six international caps for England, midfielder Brian Talbot's only major football successes came with the FA Cup. He scored in Arsenal's thrilling 3-2 win over Manchester United in the 1979 FA Cup Final at Wembley, after helping Ipswich to the trophy in 1978. He was also a marathon man: at Highbury he set a then club record when he played 70 games in the 1979/80 campaign. At Ipswich he came through the youth ranks and played two seasons on loan at the Toronto Metros before making a total of 177 League appearances at Portman Road. Following a move to Highbury, Talbot rarely missed more than half a dozen games a season and helped the Gunners to another FA Cup Final and the European Cup Winners' Cup Final in 1980, though the club lost both games. Diminishing returns at Watford (1985-1986), Stoke (1986-1988), West Brom as player-manager (1988-1991), Fulham (1991) and finally Aldershot (1991) closed his career.

NOW Currently the manager of Marsaxlokk in Malta. Talbot worked as the Chairman of the PFA (1984-1988) during his playing career and temporarily took the manager's position while at Aldershot. A full-time role was later offered to him at Maltese club Hibernians in 1991, but by 1997 he was back in England as a coach at Rushden and Diamonds (1997-2004) and was later appointed manager. Left to take charge of Oldham Atheltic (2004-2005), Oxford United (2005-2006) and Marsaxlokk in 2006, where he claimed the Premier title in his first full season. 'It's always nice to be a winner,' he says. 'To do it again with a different club is very special. Marsaxlokk have got a lot of good players, but even the people behind the club have done their part.'

Brian Talbot
ARSENAL

86 MARK ROBINS

Manchester United, Norwich City, Leicester City, Reading (loan), Deportivo Ourense (Spain), Panionios (Greece), Manchester City, Walsall, Rotherham United, Bristol City (loan), Sheffield Wednesday • 1986-2004

BORN 22 December 1969

POSITION Forward

HONOURS Manchester United: FA Cup Winner, 1990. Leicester City: Coca-Cola Cup Winner 1997

THEN Despite playing for a raft of clubs during his 18 year career, Mark Robins is best remembered for the work he did at his first two teams – Manchester United and Norwich City. Having been a product of the United youth system, he reportedly saved the bacon of manager Alex Ferguson when he scored the winning goal in the 1990 FA Cup tie against Nottingham Forest. According to paper reports, Fergie's position was apparently under threat, though his team later went on to lift the trophy that same year (Robins also scored the winner in the semi-final against Oldham Athletic). He later moved to Norwich for £800,000 where he scored on the opening game of the season against Arsenal and helped the Canaries qualify for a European spot. Injury hampered his career and by 1995 he was on a long journey which started at Leicester City (where he made two sub appearances in Leicester's victorious Coca-Cola Cup Final and subsequent replay in 1997) and finished at Conference side Burton Albion in 2005, with stops at Spain and Greece.

NOW In February 2005, Robins was appointed assistant manager at Rotherham. Later became full-time manager in 2007, though he promised not to emulate the style of some of his more experienced coaches. 'You can't be like anyone else,' he says. 'Of course you pick things up along the way, but in management you've got to be yourself otherwise the players see through you. Since I was a boy, I've always thought about the game and now I have the chance to do things my way. I want commitment, passion and quality.'

Mark Robins
MANCHESTER UNITED

87 ERIC GATES

Ipswich Town, Sunderland, Carlisle United • 1972-1991

BORN 28 June 1955

POSITION Striker

HONOURS Ipswich Town: FA Cup Winner 1978, UEFA Cup Winner 1981. Sunderland: Division Three Champions 1988

THEN A club favourite, Eric Lazenby Gates was a man of few transfers. Having signed for Ipswich Town in 1972, he helped Bobby Robson's side to an FA Cup win and European glory, while scoring 73 goals in 296 League appearances for the club. Gates also made two England appearances in 1980, though his international career was restricted by a clutch of preferred strikers, including Kevin Keegan and Ipswich team-mate Paul Mariner. Later moved to Sunderland in 1985 for £150,000 (Newcastle were interested, though it was reported that Sunderland had offered £100 a week more). The Black Cats were relegated to the Third Division in 1987, their lowest ever League position, though thankfully Gates was on hand to make amends and he forged an impressive partnership with Marco Gabbiadini – the duo scored 42 goals in one season. Sunderland bounced back immediately as champions in 1988 and Gates eventually retired in 1991 following a season at Carlisle. 'I was lucky to have the career that I did,' he says. 'And it was a privilege to play for England and Ipswich.'

NOW Having previously worked in radio, Gates currently runs High Fallowfield Farm in Durham with his partner. 'I've grown into it,' he says. 'We've got pigs, hens and sheep and I never thought I'd get into something like this, but my partner is into it. She inherited the farm from her father, and I got into it that way. It's mainly arable farming here now – wheat, barley and rape – but we've got 80 pigs as well. It's a healthy business and it's fun. It's giving me contentment. I can get up whenever I want and have a wander around the farm – there's 350 acres here, but we have contractors who do most of the work. I just potter around.'

Eric Gates
IPSWICH TOWN

88 CRAIG JOHNSTON

Middlesbrough, Liverpool • 1978-1988

BORN 25 June 1960

POSITION Midfielder/striker

HONOURS Liverpool: Division One Champions 1982, 1983, 1984, 1986, 1988; League Cup Winner 1983, 1984; FA Cup Winner 1986; European Cup Winner 1984

THEN With Brian May hair and a busybody mentality on the field ('I'd run around like a f**king lunatic,' he says), Australian Craig 'Skippy' Johnston became a crowd favourite at Anfield. Having started his career at 'Boro, he was transferred to Liverpool in 1981 for £650,000. Sadly, his versatility counted against him – as a midfielder/striker, Johnston was sometimes sidelined in favour of more established players. That said, he was pivotal in a number of trophy campaigns throughout his career, most notably the treble year of 1984 as Liverpool nabbed the League, League Cup and European Cup. More impressively, he wrote the lyrics to Liverpool's stab at pop success, Anfield Rap. Retired prematurely in 1988, though the reasons were clear: Johnston wanted to care for his seriously ill sister after she'd nearly died during a gassing accident in Morocco. Made his final appearance as a sub in the 1988 FA Cup Final defeat against Wimbledon.

NOW After his controversial departure from Anfield, Liverpool froze his assets and threatened to sue him for breach of contract. Undeterred, Johnston became a business whizz. He turned to TV production and devised an Australian gameshow called The Main Event; he made a prototype of the Predator football boot which helped to revitalise the Adidas brand, and he later developed a spiky football boot design called The Pig which nearly won him the 2004 British Design Museum's Designer of the Year Award. His latest scheme, a coaching project called Supaskills, has yet to match his previous successes. Despite acclaim it was blocked by the FA and has cost Johnston £1.5 million. 'I lost most of what I had,' he says. 'But when you're a pioneer you usually end up with arrows in your back.'

Craig Johnston
LIVERPOOL

89 ALAN DEVONSHIRE

West Ham, Watford • 1976-1992

BORN 13 April 1956

POSITION Midfielder

HONOURS West Ham: FA Cup Winner 1980

THEN There was something of the swashbuckler about Hammers midfielder, Alan Devonshire. Maybe it was the flowing locks and 'tache that contributed to his romantic image. Maybe it was his widescreen passing and elegant style of football that drew comparisons to Upton Park and England legend Trevor Brooking. Either way, with 358 League appearances (which featured 29 goals) between 1976 and 1990, the East End club certainly saw the best of this exciting talent. He even picked up eight caps along the way, playing on the left side for England. Not a bad return for a player who began business as a fork lift driver for vacuum cleaner company, Hoover. His career highlight came in 1980, however, when he lined up alongside Billy Bonds and Paul Allen in the FA Cup Final victory over Arsenal. This was his only cup glory and Devonshire ended his career at Watford in 1991/1992.

NOW Devonshire now operates in non-League football, where he first became manager of Maidenhead before taking charge of Hampton & Richmond Borough, now in the Conference South. 'I've been here four seasons now,' he says. 'I packed up playing for four or five years after my retirement and then I started a football summer school in Osterley. I was then asked to do some coaching at Maidenhead. It can be difficult at the low level but I've been quite successful. I really enjoy it. If I wasn't passionate about it I wouldn't do it. When I went to Maidenhead they going nowhere and hadn't won anything in 26 years. When I left they'd played seven cup finals in seven years – winning five of them. I've done the same at Hampton: they were relegated and I've brought them up two divisions. I still get lots of letters from the West Ham fans, which is great, but I think people still think I'm 35, I'm not, but I've lost the hair and I'm putting on weight.'

Alan Devonshire
WEST HAM

90 SIMON STAINROD

Sheffield United, Oldham Athletic, Queens Park Rangers, Sheffield Wednesday, Aston Villa, Stoke City, Rouen (France), Falkirk • 1975-1992

BORN 1 February 1959

POSITION Striker

HONOURS None

THEN Flamboyant forward who made his name mainly with QPR under the management of Terry Venables in the 1980s. Stainrod began his career at Sheffield United, where he filled the shirt of Scottish legend, Jimmy 'Jinky' Johnstone for his debut – a 5-0 thrashing at the hands of Spurs. 'I was Jimmy's driver and, even though I was so young, I would pick him up in my car to go to training,' says Stainrod. 'I was handy for a lift after a night out, and could get him home in one piece.' A move to Oldham (1979-1980) was followed by his spell at Loftus Road, where he helped QPR to the 1982 FA Cup Final against Spurs, though the game ended in defeat. Later became Sheffield Wednesday's then record signing at £250,000 in 1985 before spending two years at Villa (1985-1987), Stoke (1987-1988) and leaving England for Rouen in France (1989-1990) and Falkirk (1990-1992).

NOW Following player-manager spells at Dundee (1992-1993, where he won the Scottish League First Division in 1992) and Ayr United (1993-1995), Stainrod is now a football agent living in Cannes, France. Working for a company called Vantis Sports Solutions, he has been operating in this role since 1996, looking after a number of players in the French leagues. Which is handy, given that he speaks the lingo fluently. In 2002 he also became a founding member of Match Day Media, 'which has since developed into a successful new media business specialising in football stadia.'

Simon Stainrod
ASTON VILLA

91 ROBERT FLECK

Glasgow Rangers, Norwich City, Chelsea, Bolton Wanderers (Ioan), Bristol City (Ioan), Norwich City, Reading • 1983-1999

BORN 11 August 1965

POSITION Striker

HONOURS Glasgow Rangers: Premier League Champions 1987

THEN Despite a £2.1 million move to Chelsea in 1992, 'Flecky' is best remembered for his first spell at Carrow Road where he linked up with the 6ft 3in Robert Rosario in attack. Certainly his time at Norwich was eventful. Following on from a £580,000 transfer from Rangers in 1987, the striker endured more headlines in four years than most experience in a career: four knee operations, broken ribs, transfer speculation, club top scorer four seasons on the bounce, club fines and a less than 100% dedication to the game. 'Every Friday before a match I would have a Chinese and a couple of pints,' he says. The goals dried up at Chelsea, though his work-rate often took him all over the park – so much so that The Beatles' song Yellow Submarine was converted on the terraces to: 'Number one is Robert Fleck/Number two is Robert Fleck/Number three is Robert Fleck (and so on until) ...We all live in a Robert Fleck world, a Robert Fleck world.' He returned to Norwich in 1995 but couldn't recapture the magic. Fleck was sold to Reading for £50,000 in 1998, before retiring in February 1999 with a back injury.

NOW Currently a scout for Norwich, though he did dabble in non-League management. He teamed up with former Norwich player, Dale Gordon as a player-coach at Gorleston. He later took over the management role and steered the team to a 4-0 victory over Great Yarmouth Town in the Norfolk Senior Cup Final. In 2002, he moved to Diss Town and won the Norfolk Senior Cup in 2003 and 2005, beating Great Yarmouth Town yet again (4-1, 2003) and Wroxham (3-0, 2005). After a dreadful run of results, Fleck was sacked by Diss in October 2006. 'I always played with a smile on my face,' he says. 'Winning helps, but football is still the most enjoyable game there is, and I love it.'

Robert Fleck
GLASGOW RANGERS

92 BRIAN 'KILLER' KILCLINE

Notts County, Coventry City, Oldham Athletic, Newcastle United, Swindon Town, Mansfield Town
• 1980-1996

BORN 7 May 1962

POSITION Central defender

HONOURS Coventry City: FA Cup Winner 1987

THEN Fearsome looking centre back with a Captain Caveman-style beard and Metallica locks, Brian Kilcline is best remembered for steering Coventry City to their FA Cup Final victory over Spurs in 1987. To hinge the Cov captain's career on one moment would be unfair, however. With his tenacious tackling, never-say-die attitude and outlandish appearance, Kilcline became a cult figure wherever he played, most impressively in Kevin Keegan's improving Newcastle team (1992-1994). 'People might not expect me to talk about Brian Kilcline,' says Keegan, 'especially considering the big-name players who followed him, but he was absolutely crucial to me at the time. He settled us down and got us going.' Later played for Swindon Town (1994-1995) and Mansfield Town (1995-1996) before his retirement.

NOW Since retiring, Killer has embarked on a 'Location, Location, Location' foray into home renovations in Holmfirth, West Yorkshire, though he lives on a barge in the Midlands. Elsewhere he splits his time between charity work – he took part in the Superstars-style, 2006 Borneo Cup in Malaysia, which helped to raise funds for Children Today. Here he competed alongside former Everton 'keeper Neville Southall in several events, including white water rafting. He is also reported to have pursued a brief career as an arm wrestler, where his only defeat was by ex-Liverpool and Spurs player, Neil Ruddock. More sensibly, he can be found working as a match statistician.

Brian 'Killer' Kilcline
COVENTRY CITY

93 NEIL WEBB

Reading, Portsmouth, Nottingham Forrest, Manchester United, Nottingham Forest, Swindon Town (loan), Grimsby Town
• 1980-1997

BORN 30 July 1963

POSITION Midfielder

HONOURS Nottingham Forest: League Cup Winner 1989. Manchester United: FA Cup Winner 1990; UEFA Cup Winners' Cup Winner 1991; League Cup Winner 1992

THEN For a while, Neil Webb seemed to have it all. He made his debut at the age of 16 for Reading in the early 1980s (22 goals in 72 appearances), before joining Portsmouth where he soon caught the eye of Brian Clough and Nottingham Forest. Following his transfer in 1985, Webb became an England international and much-respected midfielder with an ability to unlock defences with his passing range and vision. By 1989, he moved to Old Trafford for £1.5 million where he helped form the beginning of Fergie's trophy haul. Sadly, injury and the presence of Paul Ince and Bryan Robson impinged on his appearances. The slide soon followed. He returned to Forest, but could not recapture his football mojo, making only 30 appearances between 1992 and 1996. He was loaned to Swindon in between (1994) and eventually moved to Grimsby in 1996, before retiring from the professional game.

NOW After retiring, Webb embarked on a couple of coaching jobs – he was player-coach at non-League Weymouth Town and in 2001 he became manager of Reading, though this didn't last long. Webb became a postman soon after. 'It's good exercise and I'm home by lunch,' he said at the time. 'It's a job, what do people expect me to do?' He later worked in the Reading promotion department and occasionally plays in the Masters, though he hasn't kept in touch with all his Forest team-mates due to work commitments. 'Football is like that,' he says. 'You are close pals and then the job takes you elsewhere. I live in Reading and Stuart Pearce didn't live far away. We joined Forest at around the same time and became friends, but it can be hard to keep in touch in football.'

Neil Webb
MANCHESTER UNITED

94 CHRIS WADDLE

Newcastle United, Tottenham Hotspur, Olympique Marseille (France), Sheffield Wednesday, Falkirk, Bradford City, Sunderland, Burnley, Torquay United • 1980-1998

BORN 14 December 1960

POSITION Winger

HONOURS Olympique Marseille: French First Division Champions 1990, 1991, 1992

THEN Despite his lolloping frame, 'Widdly' could often confuse the most adept of full backs with his deft stepovers and fancy footwork. Having worked in a sausage factory and played for Tow Law Town, he was snapped up by Newcastle in 1980. Five years and 46 League goals later, he made a big-money move to Spurs (1985-1989) for £590,000. England call-ups followed (62 in total): Waddle was in the squad for Mexico '86 and infamously missed a penalty in the semi-final shootout against West Germany in Italia '90. With his continental 'mullet' hairstyle, a move abroad seemed inevitable. French side, Olympique Marseille (1989-1992) came calling with £4.5 million and Tottenham could not refuse, though clearly it was a match made in heaven – during his three years at the club, Waddle earned three League Winners' medals and was a contender for the 1991 European Football Writers' Player of the Year. He returned to England with Sheffield Wednesday (1992-1996) and scooped the PFA Player of the Year Award in 1993, the same year he earned a runners-up medal in the FA Cup and League Cup. Closed his career with stints at Falkirk (1996), Bradford (1996-1997), Sunderland (1997), Burnley (1997-1998) and Torquay (1998).

NOW Living near Chesterfield, Waddle is a media pundit, working mainly for Radio Five Live. 'I get to co-commentate on about 20 games a season,' he says. 'I enjoy it, I do a lot of Premiership games and I'll do the England games. If we qualify for the major international tournaments, I go to them too.' He is currently striving to improve his golf handicap. 'I didn't play much when I was a footballer,' he says. 'But I love it now. I try to get on the course a couple of times a week and I go to Spain to play sometimes. I have played with Gazza – he's really good around the greens, but his driving's not so great.'

Chris Waddle
ENGLAND

95 TONY GALVIN

Tottenham Hotspur, Sheffield Wednesday, Swindon Town • 1978-1989

BORN 12 July 1956

POSITION Winger

HONOURS Tottenham Hotspur: FA Cup Winner 1981, 1982; UEFA Cup Winner 1984

THEN The most unusual of Tottenham's cup-hungry team of the early 1980s, mainly because Galvin possessed a BA (Hons) in Russian Studies. It was this academic background that made him an alien concept to the school playground's sticker-swapping hordes ('What's a BA?'), more so than even the Argentinean flair of Ossie and Ricky, or Glenn Hoddle's mercurial brilliance. As an industrious winger, Galvin scooped three trophies with Spurs before moving to Sheffield Wednesday in 1987 and Swindon Town in 1989, while claiming 29 caps for the Republic of Ireland. And the highlights of his career? 'At club level, winning the UEFA Cup with Spurs when we defeated Anderlecht in the 1984 Final,' he says. 'For Ireland, going to the European Championship finals in 1988 when we beat England 1-0. Those two moments really stand out for me.'

NOW Galvin made the most of his educational background and now works for a government organisation called the Learning And Skills Council. 'We fund training in education for the over-16s,' he says. 'We're the body that plans and funds sixth form colleges and all further education, but we don't fund universities.' Sadly, the BA (Hons) in Russian hasn't come into use during his new career. 'But I remember the Republic of Ireland team played the USSR twice and I could understand what they were saying to each other. When I asked one of them – in Russian – if we could swap shirts at the end, he was quite dismissive.'

Tony Galvin
TOTTENHAM HOTSPUR

96 DAVID BUSST

Coventry City • 1992-1996

BORN 30 June 1967

POSITION Central defender

HONOURS None

THEN Then Coventry defender, David Busst will live long in the memory as the player who endured one of the most horrific injuries in English football. Following a collision with Manchester United defender Denis Irwin at Old Trafford in 1996, he suffered a compound fracture of the fibula and tibia. 'I slid in with Brian McClair and Denis Irwin,' he says. 'I managed to get my toe to the ball first … and that's when the screaming started.' For weeks afterwards, the sports pages were filled with gruesome images of Busst's mangled leg, complete with splashes of gore. This proved to be an abrupt ending to a promising career. Having moved to Highfield Road from non-League Moor Green in 1992, Busst began establishing himself in the heart of the Coventry defence. Following his transfer, he began his charge towards first-team regularity – Busst made 50 League appearances, scoring two goals before that horrific accident cut short his career.

NOW Busst can still be found at Coventry City, where he works on the Football In The Community programme, helping to coach school children in the local area. Elsewhere, he has started a career in management: he began as manager of Solihull Borough, before resigning in 2003. He later took charge at Southern League side, Evesham United. 'As a manager I have lots of ambitions,' he says. 'And would obviously like to work at the very top level. In this game, however, you need a mate to get a good job and bring you in and none of my mates have a good job yet.' Though he competes in charity games and testimonials, his playing career is long over. In total, Busst suffered 22 operations in two years to correct the injury of 1996.

David Busst
COVENTRY CITY

97 JULIAN DICKS

Birmingham City, West Ham, Liverpool, West Ham • 1986-1999

BORN 8 August 1968

POSITION Left back

HONOURS None

THEN Fearsome left back who could be found tearing down the flanks at West Ham and Liverpool. Dicks was a fans' favourite who drew cheers with his ferocious tackling and take-no-prisoners attitude. Such was his tenacity that he was nicknamed 'The Terminator' by supporters, though this didn't help his scrappy disciplinary record – he was sent off on a number of occasions during his career. Following his arrival at Birmingham City, Dicks was transferred to Upton Park in 1988 for £300,000. He settled quickly, but his aggressive style was marked by injury and cards – during the Hammers' promotion season of 1993, Dicks missed 13 games through suspension (he was even stripped of his captaincy by manager, Billy Bonds). He later moved to Anfield in a swap deal in 1993, though his career nose-dived with recurring knee problems. Returned to Upton Park in 1994 for his final hurrah, saving the Hammers from relegation in 1996/1997 with some vital goals and impressive last ditch tackling.

NOW Following attempts to become a professional golfer (knee injuries put paid to any realistic ambition), Dicks returned to football with non-League Canvey Island. He later became the proprietor of the Shepherd and Dog pub in Langham, Essex before moving out to Spain. 'We moved out there in January, 2007. It's a different way of life but it's an amazing place and the weather's fantastic,' he says. 'I've no plans to come back. With my knee problems there would be times in the winter that I'd struggle to even get down the stairs in England, but here it's totally fine. It's nice to wake up with the sun shining, too.'

Julian Dicks
WEST HAM

98 BOBBY BARNES

West Ham, Scunthorpe United (loan), Aldershot, Swindon Town, Bournemouth, Northampton Town, Peterborough United, Partick Thistle, Torquay, Hendon, Uhlsport Rangers (Hong Kong) • 1980-1995

BORN 17 December 1962

POSITION Striker

HONOURS Aldershot: Fourth Division Play-off Winner 1987

THEN David 'Bobby' Barnes' story was one of unfulfilled promise. Having started his career at Upton Park, he drew envious glances from youth team coaches across the country, winning an FA Youth Cup for the Hammers and seven England youth caps. Things started well in his professional career too. Having signed professional terms in 1980, he scored on his debut in a 3-2 win over Watford. From then on in, Barnes' career became a long-winded journey. He made only 43 appearances in six seasons for West Ham before being loaned to Scunthorpe United (six games, no goals) and transferred to Aldershot in 1986. Here he helped the club win the first ever Fourth Division play-off in 1987. Stints at Swindon Town (1987-1989), Bournemouth (1989), Northampton Town (1989-1992) and Peterborough (1992-1993) followed, before Barnes moved to Scotland with Partick Thistle (1995), and then Torquay United (1995), Hendon (1995) and finally Hong Kong with Uhlsport Rangers.

NOW Barnes is currently the PFA's Assistant Chief Executive. 'I joined the Professional Footballers' Association in a financial capacity about eight years ago,' he says. 'And now I'm Assistant Chief Executive. I did the financial qualifications when I was a player and when I finished playing I worked as a financial Adviser on "The Outside" for a little bit. It was hard work but I enjoyed it. I then worked with former West Brom player, Brendon Batson – who was Financial Manager – at the Professional Footballers' Association as a financial consultant in 1996. Basically I went over to the general side, which involves anything from representation of players, lobbying Parliament for contractual rights and pension rights. It's important that our point of view is heard.'

Bobby Barnes
WEST HAM

99 MARK CHAMBERLAIN

Port Vale, Stoke City, Sheffield Wednesday, Portsmouth, Brighton & Hove Albion, Exeter City
• 1979-1996

BORN 19 November 1961

POSITION Winger

HONOURS None

THEN Brother of fellow Port Vale player Neville, Mark Chamberlain was a proficient winger who went on to represent England at schoolboy, Under 21 and full level (eight caps). He emerged at Vale and eventually made his full debut at the end of the 1978/79 season against Barnsley. By 1981/82, he was an ever-present in the side and was soon sold to Stoke City in August 1982. A promising England career began soon afterwards – he even played against Brazil in the Maracana stadium, which he now describes as a career highlight. 'John Barnes scored his famous solo goal,' he says. 'It was brilliant. To go there and beat Brazil was fantastic, but the pitch was crap.' Despite his speed and skill, Chamberlain only made a handful of international appearances afterwards and later moved to Sheffield Wednesday (1985-1988), Portsmouth (1988-1994), Brighton (1994) and Exeter (1995-1996).

NOW Began his post-football career by establishing soccer schools and working with handicapped children. 'I'm a youth worker in the Southampton area working with children with challenging behaviour,' he says. 'I got that through Southampton Football Club a while back, but I also work with the Southampton Academy. Working with the kids can be quite challenging – it's good fun, but it can get you down when you can't change their behaviour in the way that you would like. I go into schools and coach – the funding has gone because Southampton aren't in the Premiership anymore, but my bosses are happy with what I'm doing so they've kept me on. We just need to get some more money.'

Mark Chamberlain
PORTSMOUTH

100 SIMON BARKER

Blackburn Rovers, Queens Park Rangers, Port Vale • 1982-2000

BORN 4 November 1964

POSITION Midfielder

HONOURS None

THEN 'Tasty' midfielder who was renowned for his tough tackling, Barker came to prominence at Blackburn Rovers in the 1983/84 season where he made 28 appearances, scoring three goals. After five seasons he transferred to QPR for £400,000 in 1988. Having made his debut against Manchester United (a 0-0 draw), Barker went on to become a first-team regular until he left the club in 1998. He soon secured an 18-month contract at Port Vale. Typically, he returned to haunt the West London side when he scored against them at Loftus Road. 'I remember when I scored the goal, it was at the Loft End and I spun away shouting "Yes!" with fists pumping,' he says. 'Then I found myself looking at the Loft and I put my hand out as if to say sorry, which I've never done in my life before.'

NOW Currently works as the fancily-titled Senior Head of Delegate Liasion at the Professional Footballers' Association. 'While I was playing, I was the PFA delegate at all my clubs,' he says. 'I really enjoyed looking after the interests of the players when I was still playing myself. I was very much a PFA man – I would organise meetings at the clubs and help the players with their problems. I've been in this job for seven and-a-half years now. My day-to-day role? I'm a jack of all trades, master of none. I basically advise players on regulations and contracts; I represent players at disciplinary tribunals and I go round to all the clubs and have meetings with players where I tell them of the various benefits and services provided by the PFA. It's interesting work. But I don't miss the insecurities of football – the worry when you come to the end of your contract and the injuries – that was never enjoyable.'

Simon Barker
QUEENS PARK RANGERS

101 PAUL BIRCH

Aston Villa, Wolverhampton Wanderers, Preston North End (loan), Doncaster Rovers, Exeter City
• 1980-1999

BORN 20 November 1962

POSITION Midfielder

HONOURS None

THEN Versatile midfielder who could play on the right or middle of the park, Paul Birch began his career as an apprentice at Villa Park. While the first team strode towards League and European glory, he remained a peripheral figure, only staking his place in the side in later years. He eventually moved from Villa after 11 years of service (having lifted the 1980 FA Youth Cup and European Super Cup in 1982), playing first for Wolves (1991-1996), Preston (1996), Doncaster Rovers (1996-1997) and Exeter (1997-1999). 'The highlight of my career was probably playing so long without picking up a major injury,' he says. 'There are too many games to pick out as highlights, but I scored some goals along the way. I still get recognised a lot, but then I guess I played for some big clubs in my career.'

NOW Currently works for a company called AmeyMouchel – an Incident Support Unit on the motorways on the M42 and the M6. 'It's shift work,' he says. 'So it's four days on, four days off. Basically we have a main route which we control and maintain – that could be helping out with road traffic accidents and filling in potholes on the road. We basically make sure the motorway is operating properly. We get called out and respond to any calls within 20 minutes. I got into it through a friend who already works on the ISU. I've been doing it for a little while now. You see some strange things on the motorway and I've seen a few crashes, but nothing too bad. If there's a crash, we'll liaise with the police and they'll tell us what to clean up and what to do. But it's actually a very enjoyable job – you're doing something different every day.' Birch also plays football for the Villa Old Boys team.

Paul Birch
WOLVERHAMPTON WANDERERS

Acknowledgments

Just as filling a sticker book with all your favourite players takes time, luck and a hell of a lot of help from your friends, so this book couldn't have been completed without the help from the following...

Interviews: Ricky Villa, John Wark, Jeremy Goss, Marco Gabbiadini, Dale Gordon, Steve Ogrizovic, Paul Parker, Cyrille Regis, Mickey Thomas, Gary Gillespie, Dave Bennett, Luther Blissett, Imre Varadi, Joey Jones, Ossie Ardiles, Glenn Cockerill, Chris Waddle, Danny, Rod and Ray Wallace, Phil Neal, Arthur Albiston, Clayton Blackmore, Viv Anderson, Micky Hazard Paul Mariner, Gary Mabbutt, Mark Dennis, Mel Sterland, Jimmy Case, Ian Callaghan, Graham Baker, Malcolm Macdonald, Ronnie Whelan, Steve Nicol, Bernie Slaven, Martin Hayes, Jan Molby, Paul Allen, Terry Fenwick, David Speedie, Saint... and Greavsie, Mickey Gynn, Steve Foster, Colin Pates, Des Bremner, Graeme Sharp, Kevin Sheedy, Eric Gates, Alan Devonshire, Tony Galvin, Bobby Barnes, Mark Chamberlain, Simon Barker, and Paul Birch.

Leads, tips and info: *FourFourTwo*, Truegreats.com, *Observer Sports Monthly*, *Hotspur*, Chelsea.net, *Daily Telegraph*, exhammers.com, ww.premierleague.com, Wikipedia.org, the Leeds United official programme, www.thefa.com, Louis Massarella and Nick Moore at *FourFourTwo*, Terry Baker, the QPR press office, and the former Aston Villa Players society.

Morale support, refreshments and general encouragement: Nick Moore, 'Auntie' Phoebe Sinclair, The Potters, Dave Simmons, Warren 'Action' Jackson, Dave Croghan, Aaron Brown, Tatiana Okorie, Katherine Green, Johnny Cigarettes, iMac, Steve 'Ton Machine' Phillips and all at the Gentlemen's International Poker Organisation, all at Gentlemen's Wednesday five-a-side: Basskamp, Kevin and Pete Liffen, Biscoe Inferno, Southy, Pete Lombard Direct, Rob and Will O'Sullivan, Merse, Krankie, Cif. And of course, the family: The Dodds, The Hiltons, Ron Humm and mum, dad, Katie and Joanna.

Picture credits